HOW TO MEDITATE

Easily, Effectively & Deeply

Tahlia Newland

How to Meditate Easily, Effectively & Deeply
Tahlia Newland
Escarpment Publishing
Copyright © Tahlia Newland 2016
ISBN:9780987627209
Revised 2023

All rights reserved. No part of this book may be reproduced in any form or by any electronic or mechanical means, including information storage and retrieval systems, without permission in writing from the publisher at http://aiapublishing.com

This book employs Australian/UK spelling and punctuation conventions.

Contents

Foreword 1
Introduction 5
How to use this book 8
Why Meditate? 11
What Is Meditation? 19
Correct Posture and Why It's Important 27
What is Mind? 34
Motivation and Inspiration 38
Simply Being: The Simple and Ultimate Approach 45
Simply Breathing 51
Simply Seeing 57
Simply Listening 61
Simply Watching 66
Simply Walking 75
Simply Mantra 84
Simply Imagining 92

Simply Healing 97
Simply Loving 105
Simply Aware - Beyond a Focus 112
Establishing a Regular Practice 125
Integration: Stop Now and Meditate 135
What Next? 139
How to Evaluate a Meditation Teacher 142
And Now … 146
About the Author 147
Glossary 149

Foreword

The masked character, dressed in robes of maroon and gold, hobbled onto the stage. I had never seen a mask like it before. A plain grey diamond shape, its top peak sat a hand span above the monk's face, and the bottom peak dipped the same distance below. Though stiff, the mask's material fell like fabric over the face, giving the appearance that this old person peered through slits in some kind of veil.

Accompanied by a mantra set to music, the masked character sat slowly, as an elderly person would, on the chair set in the centre of the stage, then raised her head and revealed that the mask was, in fact, a hat. What had appeared to be the face, was actually the top of the hat. The performer's arms rose smoothly and pushed the hat to the back of her head, revealing the painted underside and, at the same time, uncovering a second mask—this one set on the performers face. The old man mask had transformed into an ornate mask of gold and copper with the hat now a diamond-shaped halo.

I watched entranced, along with one hundred or so others, as the character stood tall and left the makeshift stage without the stoop and hobble that had marked her entrance. The transformation was complete.

I discovered that this performance was entitled *The Richness Inside* and the performer was Tahlia Newland, the author of this book. She told me that the performance aimed to show that what we think of as ourselves is just a veil which shrouds our true self, a self which is more glorious than we can presently imagine. This book has essentially the same message, but here she shows us how, through the practice of meditation, we can take the first steps in uncovering this true self.

I met Tahlia, and saw the performance, at one of the Rigpa Australia Annual retreats with Sogyal Rinpoche. She instructed as part of the retreat team there for several years. I recall how her clear instructions and enthusiasm for meditation inspired large groups of students. She is a natural teacher, and before and after her career in the performance arts, she taught in both primary and secondary schools.

When I had a chance over the course of several years to talk with her, I discovered that though she became a student of Buddhism in 1996, she had studied the power of the mind and practised meditation since the early 80s, primarily working with the Seth Teachings channelled through Jane Roberts.

Tahlia spent twelve years in partial home retreat during which she studied the Buddhist teachings and practised meditation for around four hours a day, completing the preliminary and several advanced Vajrayana practices.

In 1999 Tahlia trained as a meditation instructor for Rigpa Australia and remained an instructor until she left Rigpa in June 2017. During that time, she set up and for twelve years was the Teaching Services Director of Rigpa Australia's Distance Education Centre—also known as the Bush Telegraph. She has instructed all levels of students, both in face-to-face situations and also via Skype.

Tahlia once confessed to me that she never wanted a religion, and yet she has studied and practised the Tibetan Buddhist tradition diligently, so she is well acquainted with both the subject matter and the attitude of people for whom this book has been written—those who do not want a religion but do want the essential wisdom that comes from this great tradition. This, along with her skill as an author, makes her uniquely qualified to write this book which I highly recommend. *How to Meditate* will indeed help you to meditate easily, deeply and effectively.

Dr Ian Gawler OAM, Author of *Meditation, an In-depth Guide* and *The Mind that Changes Everything*

Introduction

Imagine a diamond, pure, clear and sparkling, but covered by a layer of mud. No matter how much mud accumulates around that diamond, the diamond itself is never stained by the mud. It can always be washed off because the mud is not part of the nature of the diamond. Your true nature is the diamond, but you don't see that because it's covered in mud. You see the mud and think that's who you are.

Imagine seeing the diamond at the core of your being and knowing that that is who you are, not the mud that obscures its glorious shine. This, among other things, is what meditation can do for you. Meditation done effectively leads much further than simply relieving stress and calming the mind, it can take you to the essence of who you really are, and what you'll find there is much more powerful, inspiring, clear, vast, peaceful and compassionate than you can ever imagine when you're in your ordinary mind.

If that sounds like it's beyond you, the good news is that, with the right kind of instruction, it's not actually that difficult to have a glimpse of this true nature. Why?

Because it is your true nature. It's always with you, always there. It is who you truly are. The mud obscuring that true nature—your thoughts and emotions—just has to fall away, and since it's not part of your nature—which is like the diamond—that can actually happen quite easily if you approach it the right way.

Hence this book is about how to meditate easily, effectively and deeply. Deeply comes from meditating effectively, and effectively comes from meditating with ease. Ease is paramount. Meditation is a process of letting go, not one of effort and struggle; but to avoid struggle, we need to understand exactly what we're doing. We need to know that we're not trying to change the diamond at the core of our being, we're just letting the mud that covers it dry, crack and fall away.

Meditation study and practice go together; they inform each other. Knowledge helps you to meditate effectively, and practice helps you to understand what the points of knowledge refer to. The two together lead to experience and realisation—realisation of your true nature.

So this book starts with the knowledge you need to make sure that your meditation rests on a solid foundation. I look at the reasons why meditation is good for you, what mind and meditation actually are, motivation and, of course, correct posture. Then I lay out different methods of meditation, including loving kindness and healing meditation. I end with tips to help you establish a daily practice and chapters on how to integrate, what to look for in a teacher and where to go next.

Background

My primary meditation teacher, Sogyal Rinpoche, turned out to be a deeply flawed person, and I ceased to be his student after I discovered that he physically, emotionally and sexually abused his close students. I also discovered that those running his organisation, Rigpa, the group of which I was a part, enabled his abusive behaviour in the name of devotion. I soon realised that I had unknowingly been in a destructive cult for two decades, but it took the revelations of abuse and my studying cult and domestic abuse dynamics for the veil of ignorance to fall from my eyes. Then when most other masters of the Tibetan Buddhist religion not only failed to censure his behaviour but also appeared to see nothing wrong with it, I left the religion, vowing never to fall into organised religion again.

For the full story of Sogyal Lakar's abuse of power and what went wrong in Rigpa, see my book *Fallout: Recovering from Abuse in Tibetan Buddhism*.

Despite all this, I was able, in those two decades, to study and practice the Dzogchen teachings on the subtle-most nature of mind, the 'highest' teachings of the Tibetan Buddhist tradition. Despite his personal faults, Sogyal Lakar (Rinpoche) faithfully taught Dzogchen as it was taught to him by the great Dzogchen master Nyoshul Khen Rinpoche, and for his diligent transmission of those teachings I am extremely grateful. That Dzogchen training gives me the confidence to write this book.

Though I have rejected the religion, the power of the practices themselves remains unassailable for me, as they speak to the very nature of my own being as I experience it. Remove the feudal structure, the blind devotion, the gurus who prey on students desperate to gain enlightenment at any cost, and the uncorrected misunderstandings that come from surface study and biased minds, and you have a highly valuable system of meditation practice. It is this essential aspect of the Tibetan tradition, pared of its failings, that remains with me and inspires the content of this book.

The aim of my life, known and expressed from an early age, is to bring benefit to beings in whatever way my talents and abilities enable, and I hope that this book will be of benefit to those who read it.

How to use this book

Though short, this book is a complete guide to meditation. To get the most out of it, read it slowly to allow the words to sink in, and afterwards give yourself time to consider what you've read. Then put it into practice.

If we don't consider the words of a teaching, see if they resonate with us, and check them out in our meditation practice, they aren't that much use to us. It's like when you put food in your mouth, you have to chew it over and swallow it if you want the nourishment the food can provide.

If you have a daily meditation practice already, then consider this a refresher: words to remind you of what you know, fill gaps in your knowledge and inspire and deepen your meditation. If you're new to meditation, then this book will get you started. Many of the middle chapters—simply being, simply breathing and so on—include guided practices, so you can sit in meditation posture and practice as you read.

You could read a section through at night (they're short) and the next morning, read it again to inform or guide your meditation. Read it as meditation. Practise focusing without distraction on the words and allow them to inspire your mind into peace and clarity.

It's worthwhile to understand also, though I have written them into sentences, the words and phrases used in the core information are not my words. They are the same words passed down from master to master in the Tibetan tradition. Though they are framed in a modern context, I use the same words because those words have power—the power to transform. So use this book in a way that allows that power to resonate in your being.

Though I've tried to stick to ordinary language rather than use Buddhist terminology, where Buddhist terms are used, I've explained them in a glossary at the end.

You'll also find a certain amount of repetition in this book. This is intentional because we often need to hear some of these ideas repeated before we really get them.

Why Meditate?

Anyone with any meditation experience knows that it's good for them, but what does science say? Here are seven reasons to meditate according to research on the benefits of meditation. The body of evidence is growing all the time, and what I list here is only some of it.

1. It's good for your health

- **Helps lower blood pressure** – According to findings published in the Journal of Psychosomatic Medicine, use of a Mindfulness-Based Stress Reduction (MBSR) technique resulted in substantial and statistically significant reductions in blood pressure – a 4.8-mm Hg reduction in systolic blood pressure (SBP) and a 1.9-mm Hg reduction in diastolic blood pressure (DBP).
- **Increases immune function** – A study on alterations in brain and immune function produced by mindfulness meditation published in the Journal of

Psychosomatic Medicine, July 2003 – Volume 65 – Issue 4 – p 564–570, concluded: These findings demonstrate that a short program in mindfulness meditation produces demonstrable effects on brain and immune function. These findings suggest that meditation may change brain and immune function in positive ways.

- **Decreases pain** – studies have shown a positive relationship between meditative experience and pain relief. (Grant et al., 2010, Brown & Jones, 2010.)
- **Decreases inflammation at a cellular level** – An eight-week MBSR course resulted in a significantly smaller post-stress inflammatory response. (Brain, Behaviour, and Immunity, Volume 27, January 2013, Pages 174–184.)

2. It makes you happier

- **Increases positive emotion** – Results showed that loving kindness meditation practice produced increases over time in daily experiences of positive emotions, which, in turn, produced increases in a wide range of personal resources which increased life satisfaction and reduced depressive symptoms. (Journal of Personality and Social Psychology, Vol 95(5), Nov 2008, 1045-1062)

- **Decreases depression** – Overall, results suggest that mindfulness meditation practice primarily leads to decreases in ruminative thinking, even after controlling for reductions in affective symptoms and dysfunctional beliefs. (Cognitive Therapy and Research August 2004, Volume 28, Issue 4, pp 433–455)

- **Decreases anxiety** – Group mindfulness meditation training programs effectively reduce symptoms of anxiety and panic and can help maintain these reductions in patients with generalised anxiety disorder, panic disorder, or panic disorder with agoraphobia. (American Journal of Psychiatry Volume 149, Issue 7, July 1992, pp. 936-943)

- **Decreases stress** – Results from a prospective randomised controlled pilot study suggest that an eight-week MBSR intervention may be effective for reducing stress and increasing quality of life and self-compassion in health care professionals.

3. It's good for your interactions with others

- **Increases social connection & emotional intelligence** – Loving kindness meditation, in particular, gives a greater sense of purpose and social ease, decreases illness symptoms, increases life satisfaction and reduces depressive symptoms.
- **Makes you more compassionate** – Compassion cultivation training resulted in significant improvements in all three domains of compassion—compassion for others, receiving compassion from others, and self-compassion.
- **Makes you feel less lonely** – Mindfulness meditation training reduces loneliness and pro-inflammatory gene expression in older adults. (Brain, Behavior, and Immunity, Volume 26, Issue 7, October 2012, Pages 1095-11010)

4. It gives you greater self-control

- **Improves your ability for introspection and for handling your emotions** – A randomised controlled trial of compassion cultivation training looking at mindfulness, affect and emotion regulation discovered that, generally, the ability to accept the present moment via mindful awareness and adopting a nonjudgmental stance has been associated with more tolerance of uncomfortable emotions.

5. It alters your brain in a good way

- **Increases volume of grey matter** in areas related to emotion regulation, positive emotion, self-control and paying attention.

6. It makes you more productive

- Increases your focus & attention.
- Improves your ability to multitask.
- Improves your memory.

- Improves your ability to be creative and think outside the box. See research by J. Schooler.

7. It makes you wiser and more genuine

You see more clearly, so you're more able to make wise choices. You're not a slave to your thoughts and emotions. You're less likely to react and more likely to consider the best course of action before acting. And at the ultimate level, you can come to know the true state of everything – that's real wisdom. Because your fear is less, and you're able to be 'happy in your own skin', you can be more genuine in your interactions with people. That makes you more likeable and easier to be around. You're less likely to push agendas and more likely to actually listen to other people.

What's not to like about all this?

A warning
Meditation is a tool for examining the mind and for going beyond the mind, and like all tools it can be misused.

Meditation is not a cure for mental illness. In fact, in some people, it can make mental illnesses worse and even bring on psychotic episodes—especially if not taught in a grounded fashion. Few meditation teachers have any knowledge of psychology and even fewer have the skills in psychotherapy required to assist people with mental health challenges.

There is no body which evaluates and authorises meditation teachers, not in the West or in the East. Not everyone who teaches meditation is qualified; even those who are qualified do not necessarily teach it well and unfortunately ethical conduct by meditation teachers cannot be assumed, not even by those who profess its importance. Beware of any teacher who demands your devotion. Cults easily form around charismatic teachers.

The major issue with meditation is that it can be used to bypass our emotional and physical issues, to ignore or even repress emotional pain rather than using it to assist in deep examination of our issues and feelings. Thus people can spend years studying meditation and end up still as messed up emotionally as they were before they started—or even more so. For those with traumatic backgrounds and those with a tendency to deny their feelings, a course of psychotherapy is advisable before going too deeply into meditation. For many of us psychotherapy is as important as meditation—if not more so—for our mental wellbeing.

Meditation trains you to step back, so you can, in any moment, choose whether or not to react to a thought or feeling, thus freeing you from being controlled by random thoughts. Correctly applied to one's life experience, it should bring you deeper into experience, not further away from it. It should make you more able to experience, to actually feel your painful emotions and address their cause, not less able. Learning to 'be with whatever arises' without reacting to it, should not be a method for ignoring or supressing one's gut feelings. Nor should it mean not acting to right an injustice or improve one's physical or emotional reality.

Beware of falling into the trap of thinking that there is some 'spiritual' or peaceful place or state separate to your existence as an embodied human being or thinking that meditation will solve all your problems. We have mental, emotional and physical bodies, and our aim is to be aware of the totality of our beings, not to deny inconvenient parts of ourselves in favour of some self-created illusion.

What Is Meditation?

You may think it's unnecessary to define the meaning of such a common word, but not only are there many different kinds of meditations taught throughout the world, but also meditation is something people have a lot of erroneous assumptions about. There is no point attempting to learn to do something if we don't know what exactly it is that we're trying to do. Meditating effectively requires us to have a good understanding of what meditation is and how the techniques work.

What meditation isn't
First, let's debug a few common misunderstandings. Meditation is not:

- Watching your breath or chanting mantras—they're techniques, not meditation itself.
- Getting rid of your thoughts.
- Just for religious or spiritual people.
- Just for relaxation, staying calm or releasing stress. These are results of meditation, but it can go a lot further than that.

Ah, okay; so what is meditation?

Meditation is the state of non-distraction. It's a mind that is not chasing after every thought, every sight, every sound. We can still have thoughts while in meditation. In fact, for so long as we have a mind, we will have thoughts—the ever-practical Tibetans say that having a mind without thoughts is as impossible as tea without tea leaves. What we don't do when in a state of meditation is get caught up in our thoughts—and while we're practising getting to that state, if we do get caught up, as soon as we realise it, we simply return our attention back onto the object we're focusing on, for example our breath or a mantra. The trick is not to suppress our thoughts and not to indulge in them, but to simply watch them come and watch them go, because they will go, naturally of their own accord, so long as we don't hang onto them and stir them up by thinking about them.

But ... what are we trying to be undistracted from?

This depends on your level of experience. When beginning, you'll have an object for your meditation practice—a sight, a sound, your breath—and that's what you're practising being undistracted from. After a little more experience, you may be practising being undistracted from the present moment, and if you've recognised the true nature of your mind —your inner essence—then you'll be practising being undistracted from the true nature of your mind. Recognising the true nature of your mind and resting undistracted in that state is the whole point of meditation, and all the benefits of meditation are side-effects of being in this state or close to it. To understand what I mean by the true nature of your mind, you need to understand something very important about your mind, because it may not be what you think it is.

The two aspects of mind

In the West, we tend to think of our mind as thoughts and emotions, but—and this is a very important, and for many a revolutionary, point—there are two aspects to our mind: the appearance and the essence or true nature of mind. Thoughts and emotions are not the mind itself; they are only the appearance of mind. The true nature of our mind is the open, clear and compassionate state from which our thoughts and emotions spring. One aspect is the relative mind—thoughts and emotions—and the other is the absolute mind—the calm, clear space behind those thoughts and emotions. This absolute mind is the true nature of our mind, our inner essence, and experiencing this is what we're really aiming for in meditation.

Important things to understand

- What meditation actually is, i.e., resting in the state of non-distraction.
- What you're aiming to do—ultimately to rest undistracted in the true nature of your mind, the

open, clear and responsive part you can glimpse in the gaps between your thoughts.
- The general approach—in meditation you aren't actually trying to do anything, rather you're practising not doing. You're allowing yourself to simply be, to be as you are in the moment, and to simply observe what rises and falls in your mind without getting hooked into the risings.
- The general attitude—be kind to yourself and to whatever rises in your mind. Whatever happens, it's all okay. Be like a wise old man or woman watching children at play. Watching your thoughts and emotions in this way will give you some space from them so they will no longer rule you.

Two kinds of meditation

There are two kinds of meditation, one in the domain of the conceptual or ordinary mind where we perceive a subject, an object and an action; and one in the domain of the true nature of mind, which is beyond all concepts: Shamata meditation, meaning calm abiding or peacefully remaining, stays within the conceptual mind, and Vipassyana, meaning clear seeing or special insight, moves beyond the conceptual mind—at least as it is understood in the Tibetan tradition. In other traditions, the word Vipassyana can be used to refer to the awareness aspect of Shamata meditation, which is still within the realm of the conceptual mind—if there's an object of focus in the meditation, even if it's a subtle one like the present moment, the meditation is still within the conceptual mind. But regardless of what you call it, you can meditate within the realm of the conceptual mind, or you can go beyond the conceptual mind to the place where your sense of separation dissolves and you become one with everything.

Most widely available meditation techniques work within the realm of the ordinary mind, and that's the right place to start because the idea is to stabilise the ordinary mind to provide a jumping off point for going deeper. The highest teachings on meditation are what are called Mahamudra or Dzogchen in the Tibetan tradition. I'm lucky that I have received many teachings on Dzogchen. It's truly mind-blowing stuff!

How Shamata meditation instructions 'work'

The problem with our ordinary mind is that it's constantly searching for entertainment, and this causes us to be distracted from the present moment. Our minds are most likely a whirl of thoughts that we follow blindly, wandering endlessly without awareness from one thought to the next and often stumbling around in circles that drive us crazy. This constant state of distraction makes us disconnected from the present and from our true self, and that's the real cause of stress. If we were present with ourselves instead of off in our heads somewhere, we could handle everything so much more easily.

I said earlier that the true nature of our mind can be glimpsed between our thoughts, but before we can see the gaps, we need to slow our thoughts down a bit. We need to stop our mind racing ahead and bring it into the present. The way we do that is to give our mind something to focus on, and every time our mind wanders off, when we catch ourselves, we bring it back to the thing we're focusing on. We call this thing the object of the meditation, and meditation with an object can also be called 'Shamata with support'.

Many disciplines use the breath as the object of meditation, but we can also use a visual object—either real or imagined—a sound, a chant, even thoughts, movement and the present moment as the object of our meditation. Whatever we use, the process is the same: when our mind wanders off, we bring it back to the object of our meditation—over and over and over.

At some point in the meditation our thoughts will slow down, and eventually the sense of a meditator, something to meditate on and the action of meditation will dissolve to some degree, then we're left resting in the present moment. This is called Shamata without support, and that's a good place to be. We can live our life in that state, a state of peace and clarity.

Which method is best?

With so many different kinds of meditation around, how do we know we're getting the right kind of instructions? How can we be sure that our meditation is effective, that we're getting the most out of the time we spend sitting on our cushion?

It's not so much a matter of right or wrong, but more a matter of what we want our meditation practice to do for us. Most meditation courses offered will probably assist with stress reduction and making us feel calmer—at least while we're doing the meditation—but not all of them will give us the instructions we need if we want to go deeper.

If we're just looking for something to help us sleep, then meditating with our eyes closed will be more beneficial for that purpose than meditating with our eyes open, but if we want to integrate our meditation into our daily life so that we can live every moment in peace and clarity, then meditating with our eyes open is vital.

Of course, if we learn meditation with our eyes open, there's no reason why we can't meditate with our eyes closed if we need help sleeping. In the same way, meditation instructions that will take us all the way to enlightenment will bring us the same benefits as one designed just to reduce stress plus more; so why restrict ourselves?

For going deeper, I trust those that have been working on refining their meditation instructions for thousands of years, and that have a strong lineage of passing knowledge down from teacher to pupil without distortion. Egos muddy the pure stream of transmission, so choose a tradition with safeguards in place to make sure this doesn't happen. The Tibetan way is that every teacher has his or her own teacher, and a teacher's peers keep an eye on him or her as well. The Tibetan Buddhist teachings also include all the teachings of the Buddha—the Hinayana, the Mahayana and the Vajrayana—so they have the full spectrum of knowledge. This is why I trust the instructions that came to me from this tradition—as well as my personal experience, of course.

If you're resisting the idea of using meditation instructions that come from a religion, bear in mind that the *essence* of meditation is not at all religious, even as taught by the great Tibetan masters. True meditation, what meditation really is, is beyond all religions. It transcends them all, even Buddhism.

Correct Posture and Why It's Important

Outer and inner posture

Posture is the way we hold ourselves, and when doing a formal meditation session, we take a specific posture to help us attain the meditative mind state—the state of non-distraction. There is an outer posture, the way we sit, and an inner posture, the way we hold our mind, or approach our practice. The inner posture is an attitude of spaciousness and not having any agenda. We shouldn't be trying to achieve anything; we are simply sitting and watching whatever arises. We do not evaluate or comment; we just sit with whatever is happening at that moment.

The rest of this chapter details the physical meditation posture and the reasons for it. Sitting in a certain way is important because the body is the physical support for the mind. There is a relationship between the mind and the body.

An analogy for this relationship is a glass of water on a table: the table is the body, the support, and the glass is the mind supported on that table. If we move the table about, the glass will fall over and spill the water, but if we leave the table alone, the cup will stay still.

Basically, if you sit this way, it's easier for your mind to become calm and clear.

The Seven Point Posture of Vairocana

Correct meditation posture according to the Tibetan tradition is sometimes referred to as The Seven Point Posture of Vairocana.

Point 1: Crossed legs

The traditional ideal posture is called 'the vajra posture', where the left foot rests on the right thigh, and the right foot rests on the left thigh, but few Westerners can manage that, so just sitting cross-legged with your bottom on a cushion is fine. You need to be comfortable.

If sitting cross-legged is out of the question for you, sitting on a chair is also fine. In that case, you sit with your legs uncrossed and feet flat on the floor, or you can rest your feet on a cushion and cross your ankles with your knees splayed open.

If you are able to sit in the vajra posture, that's great because it's a very stable way of sitting, but if you can't manage it or just find it uncomfortable, don't force it.

You'll only cause yourself damage, and you'll not be able to meditate. It's important not to get fixated on this point.

Point 2: Hands in your lap or on your knees

The second point of the posture is how you place your hands. There are two options: either place the hands in your lap, one resting on top of the other, just below the level of your navel; or place your hands palms down on your knees, just resting comfortably.

Point 3: Shoulders back

The third point is that there should be some space between your body and your upper arms, so that your arms are not held in close to the body. The traditional metaphor is that your arms and shoulders should be spread like a vulture's wings.

Point 4: Straight back

The fourth point is the back. The spine should be straight, but sit with ease, keeping the natural curve of the spine. If you're on a chair, a cushion at your back will help support your lumbar region so you can sit straight.

I find it helpful to imagine an angel or buddha (it could be anyone) above me holding a golden thread that runs through my spine to my tail bone. They give a gentle lift to the spine. I used to use this image to help dancers get the correct dance posture, and it gave a nice feeling of lightness and ease to their posture.

The reason a straight spine is important is because it allows the inner air (prana, or life force) to flow easily in the subtle channels of the body. A straight central channel will keep you alert. If you slump, you are more likely to fall asleep.

Point 5: Head and neck

The fifth point of the posture concerns the head and the neck. The chin should be dropped down slightly so the back of the neck is long.

The reason we do this is because two subtle channels that encourage discursive thoughts run through the neck, and lowering the chin slightly blocks those channels, which ensures that the energy within them doesn't create a lot of thoughts. It's also the best physical posture of your neck for your bodily health, but make sure that your head isn't pushed forward; the centre of your head should sit in the middle of your shoulders, aligned with your spine.

Point 6: Mouth slightly open

As in all things, there needs to be a balance here; don't let your mouth hang open, and don't clench your teeth together. Leave just the slightest space between your upper teeth and your lower teeth, so that they are almost, but not quite, touching.

Keep your mouth slightly open, as if you were about to say 'ah'.

Another recommendation is to let the tip of the tongue rest against the hard palate, behind the upper teeth. But this depends on the individual: it's a matter of choice; some people find it uncomfortable, and others find it useful.

So, with your lips just barely parted, and your teeth barely touching, let your breath move softly in and out of your mouth as you meditate. Remembering this point can also help make your meditation vivid.

Point 7: The gaze

The gaze is the way your **eyes** are looking while you're meditating.

Many people find it helpful to keep their eyes closed, and that's fine at the beginning if you need to do it to help gather, calm, settle your mind, but eventually it's best to meditate with your eyes open. So after a while, open them, just halfway—the way they usually are—and without looking at anything in particular, simply let your gaze gently rest. Some texts recommend looking downwards, past the tip of your nose—not at your nose or you'll go cross-eyed!—but to awaken and brighten up your deeper awareness, it's better to raise your gaze and look straight out into the space in front of you.

You can also alternate between these two kinds of gaze; sometimes look up, sometimes look down. If your meditation becomes sleepy or dull, bring the gaze up. If your mind becomes agitated, bring the gaze more down.

Why meditate with our eyes open:

- We are less likely to fall asleep.
- Our meditation will be brighter.
- The eyes are the door to the wisdom channels. Close them off and we make it harder for true insight to arise.
- It makes it easier for us to integrate meditation into our daily life, or meditate anywhere, anytime.

Correct meditation posture is healthy for your body as well as your mind

Each of these posture points is also an antidote for a particular emotional state, such as desire, attachment, aversion and so on.

Sitting comfortably in the meditation posture also promotes good health and physical wellbeing. If our body is twisted or cramped, the energy is blocked and that promotes illness. According to Tibetan and Indian medicine, the proper posture contributes to the harmonising of the humours and elements in the body. Also the flow of energy and blood is enhanced, which promotes long life. Research has shown that people who have meditated daily for a period of ten years or more tend to be 5 years or more younger in physical age than non-meditators of the same age according to years lived.

What is Mind?

Meditation involves working with the mind, so though I mentioned the two aspects of mind earlier, let's look at our minds in more depth.

What is mind, really? Is it just thoughts and emotions? We may think that, but mind is more than that. Consider a thought: it's not there all the time, is it? Thoughts come and go. Where do they come from? Where do they go? Think about that for a moment.

They just appear, don't they? One minute they aren't there, and the next they're there, and if we think about them, we get a whole lot more thoughts. But what if we stop thinking? You may not have experienced that, but it is possible. If you're ever relaxed enough that your thoughts slow down a bit, you might experience a gap between your thoughts. What happens to your mind during that gap? Does it not exist for a moment? Your thoughts and emotions have gone quiet, but they are only part of your mind.

The two aspects

Thoughts and emotions are just the appearance of mind, not the true nature of mind. The true nature of your mind is the limitless space from which thoughts and emotions emerge and to which they return. Thoughts are your relative mind, conditioned by circumstances, and the true nature of your mind is your absolute mind whose nature is never conditioned or compromised by circumstances.

The important thing to understand here is that the thoughts and emotions you experience are merely the radiance or appearance of the open, creative natural state of your mind. They burst into existence because of inspiration, and they fade of their own accord if we don't give them any attention, like ripples in water—they appear if you throw a stone into the water, then they fade away.

The nature of mind is like the brilliant, clear and endless blue sky, and the appearance of mind is like the clouds that obscure it when we're looking up from the ground. The thing we tend to forget is that above those clouds, the sky is always blue. It's always there, completely unaffected by the clouds. In the same way, the nature of mind is always there, unstained by thoughts and emotions; we're just usually so caught up in our thoughts and emotions that we don't see or experience this deeper reality of ourselves.

The mind of thoughts and emotions can drive us crazy. Thoughts go round and round and stir up emotions, and the more you think about those thoughts, the worse the emotions get. The true nature of mind, however, is calm and clear, and when the clouds of your ordinary mind dissolve, you can experience this true nature of your mind, a space free of anxiety and stress. Meditation is the process of clearing the clouds so we can see and experience the open nature of the sky, the space where we are always peaceful, always clear.

You can experience this for yourself. When through the practice of meditation, your thoughts slow down a little, you will come to see gaps between your thoughts. In those gaps, you'll find a clear open space that is present, peaceful and vibrant. That's what you're aiming for, resting in that space. And knowing that it's there, that those thoughts and emotions are just like clouds in a perfectly blue sky makes a huge difference to your understanding of what you're doing in meditation.

How does understanding what is mind help?

If you understand that thoughts and emotions are not the true nature of your mind, you will be less inclined to get caught up in or overwhelmed by them.

Just knowing that the true nature of your mind is clear, open and inherently peaceful can release tension. Tasting it in meditation is even more powerful.

This understanding makes meditation, and working with your mind in general, a lot easier. If you think your mind is your thoughts and emotions and you think that meditation is trying to calm those thoughts and emotions, you have a struggle because you're trying to change something, but if you think that your mind—your true mind—is already calm and clear, then all you have to do is leave your thoughts alone, and when they naturally fade—as they will if you stop chasing after them—the peace is naturally there. You're not trying to change anything; you're just undertaking a process that will slow down your thoughts enough that you can see beneath them to the mind that is always peaceful.

When the surface of a lake is still, you can see into the water to the lakebed below, but when the surface is ruffled by wind, you can't see into the water. Meditation is like calming the wind. The surface of your mind stills so you can see the natural clarity of the true nature of your mind. You don't have to change anything, just allow your mind to settle.

Motivation and Inspiration: A Frame for Our Practice

All the knowledge in the world is of no use to us if we're not motivated to use it, and knowing how to meditate is not the same as actually meditating. Clearly, to get the benefits of meditation we have to actually meditate. Otherwise, it's like having the medicine for an ailment, but not taking it; if we don't take the medicine, we won't get better.

Motivation is our prime mover. Motivation comes first, action comes second, so in order to meditate we have to be motivated to do so, and the greater the motivation, the more likely we are to meditate. If you've read this far, then I'm guessing that you really do want to meditate. Maybe you've read about the benefits of meditation, noted that the claims are backed up by scientific research and have decided that you want, or need, those benefits in your life. Great. That may be enough to get you to actually put into practice what you're learning here, but you should also know that …

Time is running out

If you keep putting it off until tomorrow, one day there won't be any tomorrow. You may die before you get your meditation practice going. Part of you might not care too much, but death is the part of life where you most need meditation.

No matter how we die, and no matter what beliefs we subscribe to around an afterlife, no one can dispute that the biggest help to us when we die will be a mind that is relaxed and able to let go. The time we most need the benefits of meditation is at the moment of our death. Nothing will help us more.

We will all die eventually. You will die. I will die. And the day you're dying is a bit late to start a meditation practice. The best scenario is that by then meditation comes so naturally to us that we can slip into a meditative state no matter what our circumstances.

Knowing this should inspire us to establish a daily meditation practice but establishing a habit for meditation—or anything else for that matter—takes discipline, and though the discipline becomes effortless after we start to feel the benefits of practice, at the beginning it does take some effort—only discipline makes it easy. A strong motivation to practise makes it easier to be disciplined and so does inspiration, and the good news is that we don't have to wait until inspiration hits us, we can set things up so that inspiration is an integral part of our practice.

Framing your practice with thoughts of others

When I first tried meditation, it tended to make me fall asleep. I felt pretty bored and dull minded, so my attempts were erratic. I wasn't that motivated, and I wasn't getting much benefit either. I soon gave up. I'd been meditating with my eyes closed, which had made me sleepy, but the aspect of the Tibetan approach that really revolutionised my practice was framing the practice with thoughts of benefiting others.

Meditating to gain the benefits of meditation for oneself is fine, and certainly better than not meditating at all, but meditating with the intention to benefit others gives our practice extra power to transcend our ordinary mind—and eventually help others to do the same.

Thinking of others expands our mind beyond the limits of thinking of just ourselves and our own welfare. And if we think of *all* sentient beings—not just those we know and love—it propels our mind into a space that encompasses everyone everywhere. That's a very spacious mind and a great way to start a meditation session.

There's a huge difference between just sitting and going straight into your practice and sitting and thinking:

> By the power and the truth of this practice:

> May all sentient beings have happiness and the causes of happiness.
>
> May they be free from suffering and the causes of suffering.
>
> May they never be separated from the great happiness devoid of suffering.
>
> And may they dwell in the great equanimity that is free from attachment and aversion.

That's the formal prayer used in Tibetan Buddhism, but we can think something as simple as 'May this practice help all beings be happy and free from suffering.' Then we can think specifically of those who are really suffering in our world.

Wanting to free all beings from suffering and bring them to the ultimate happiness of enlightenment is the motivation of a bodhisattva—a spiritual warrior who seeks enlightenment purely so that he or she will gain the wisdom, compassion and power to help others.

The bodhisattva's motivation that you set at the start of a session is one side of the frame.

In the middle, be spacious
Inside the frame is space.

During the body of our meditation, we meditate with a sense of ease and spaciousness. Best is we meditate without any sense of subject, object or action, in a state free of concepts, without any point of reference, just resting in the vast, open and compassionate state of the nature of our mind, but on a simple level, it's just not getting caught up in whatever arises in our mind. It's meditating without any agenda, without trying to achieve anything, rather with a sense of allowing the mud of our ordinary thoughts and emotions to fall away and naturally reveal the shining diamond of our true nature.

It's approaching our meditation with ease and spaciousness.

At the end

The other side of the frame is at the end of our practice. Here we dedicate the merit, or benefit, we've gained from the practice to others. We're sharing the benefit around, thinking in a larger way and developing our capacity for love and compassion. We can think something like 'May the benefit of this practice be shared with all beings, so they may be free of negative emotions and gain the ultimate happiness of enlightenment.'

Do you see how powerful this makes your practice? Can you feel it? I can. I could the very first time I framed my practice that way, and I still love that I can sit in my meditation room and actually help everyone in the universe.

Practising for all people, not just for myself, makes it easier for me to remember to practise, gives me more inspiration to practise and makes the practice itself much stronger. Helping others actually helps you.

Environmental inspiration

The natural world—a garden, a forest, by a brook, river or ocean—is an inspiring environment in which to practise, perhaps because it's so natural, so simply as it is, it invokes the same simplicity and naturalness in us.

You can also set up a cosy spot in your house or room in which to meditate. Make a place that just by entering it inspires a sense of peace and spaciousness. Make a shrine decorated with whatever you find inspiring for your practice.

And keep a book of insights, a place where you write anything you read that really speaks to you, things that inspire you. Keep it nearby and read from it on the days when you feel sluggish and uninspired. Also collect teachings that inspire you. Most meditation teachers these days have recorded teachings or guided practices that you can use to inspire and guide you. And you can find many talks by meditation teachers on YouTube—though don't take instructions from lots of different traditions or you might just confuse yourself. Also mark places in books, so you can open them and take a deep breath of inspiration when you need a little extra help to remind yourself why you really do need to STOP NOW and simply be.

Now that you understand what you're doing, have your meditation spot set up, and know how to frame your practice, you're ready to start practising.

Simply Being: The Simple and Ultimate Approach

We've looked at mind and what meditation actually is, and the correct posture and why it's important; that information, once understood and digested, gives us the basis of a strong meditation practice. Now we're going to look at one way to approach the practice of meditation, and further chapters will look at different approaches.

The 'simply being' approach to how to meditate is based on the understanding that the true nature of our mind is already calm and clear, that any wildness of thoughts and emotions is not the actual nature of our mind, but merely what obscures it. All we have to do is let those obscurations fall away and the peace and clarity of our inner essence will reveal itself naturally.

This is the approach of natural great ease. The approach where we just drop the mud that obscures our true nature. It is both simple and profound. At its deepest level, it is resting in the true nature of our mind, but even as beginners we may have a glimpse of this—or maybe not. Either way, it doesn't matter. It can be the ultimate meditation or simply a moment of release before we use one of the more conceptual approaches to meditation. The trick is to approach it with ease.

Guided meditation

So let's start by assuming a good posture.

- ➤ **Legs:** If on a cushion, cross your legs. If on a chair, put your feet flat on the floor or on a cushion.
- ➤ **Hands:** Hands in your lap, one resting on top of the other, or palms down on your knees.
- ➤ **Shoulders back:** Have some space between your body and your upper arms.
- ➤ **Back straight:** But sit with ease, keeping the natural curve of the spine.
- ➤ **Neck:** Drop your chin down slightly so the back of the neck is long.
- ➤ **Mouth slightly open** as if you're about to say 'ah'.
- ➤ **Eyes:** half open/half closed. Look down slightly and a couple of metres in front of you. Let your gaze gently rest.

Essentially, it's sitting with your spine straight and your limbs relaxed.

Now, take a breath in through your nose, then let it out through your mouth, expelling any negativity you may hold as you do so.

Release and relax your mind.

Then breathe naturally and just leave your mind in that relaxed space.

Wish that your meditation bring benefit to all beings—including yourself. Think of people you know who are suffering, then those living in world trouble spots, and then every single being in the universe. Make your mind vast and magnanimous. Think: 'May this practice help all beings be happy and free from suffering.'

Take another deep breath and, when you exhale, drop your mind.

Just drop it.

Like a stone dropped into a pool of water.

Simply be.

Don't try to do anything.

Don't try to stop thoughts or make thoughts.

Don't even try to meditate.

Just be. As you are, now, in this moment.

Whatever happens is fine.

Feel your body on your seat and your awareness in and around you, and simply be here now.

Dealing with thoughts in meditation

When thoughts arise, don't try to stop them.

Just let them come.

And let them go.

Continue to breathe naturally and let any thoughts pass through your mind like clouds in the sky.

Don't follow your thoughts. They are merely thoughts, nothing more. They have no power over you unless you give them power by engaging with them.

So don't engage with your thoughts.

Watch them pass through your mind like credits across a television screen.

If you get so caught up in your thoughts that you find it hard to extricate yourself from them, you can take another deep breath, breathe out slowly, and release and relax your mind again.

Sky and clouds

The true nature of your mind is like the sky—clear and boundless.

Thoughts and emotions are like the clouds. If you're looking up from the ground, they obscure the sky, but if you fly above the clouds, the blue sky is always there, untouched by the clouds.

Clouds eventually get blown away or dissolve into the sky. In the same way, your thoughts arise from the clear sky of your mind, then—if you leave them alone—they dissolve back into it.

So simply be.

Here.

Now.

Leave everything as it is.

And remain in that spacious, relaxed state.

Simply be.

…

At the end of the meditation, think something like, 'May the benefit of this practice be shared with all beings, so they may be free of negative emotions and gain the ultimate happiness of enlightenment.'

When you get up to go about your day, see if you can take whatever peace you've found with you.

…

These instructions may be all you need, or you may find that you have a sense of peace for a moment or two but can't sustain it, or maybe your mind was so wild that all you saw was your crazy thoughts. If you fit the latter two categories, then you're like most of the human population, and you need a more conceptual approach until your mind has calmed somewhat.

Even so, simply being is a good way to start your meditation, and end it, and also to drop into occasionally in the middle. Alternating a more conceptual approach and this simple letting go can deepen your meditation considerably.

It's also a really good idea to stop during your day and simply be for a moment or two. It will refresh your mind and your energy. You can even have a timer set on your phone to remind you. I have a meditation app that I set for an hour at a time, and every hour when the bell rings, I just stop and simply be.

Simply Breathing

All meditation techniques can be categorised into two: those with an object and those without. In meditation with an object, though the object of the meditation can vary, the basic premise is the same: we focus our mind on the object, and when our mind wanders off somewhere else, we bring it back to the object. The process of bringing our mind back to one object over and over again settles the ordinary thinking mind and allows the fog to clear, and thus reveal our innate peace and clarity.

Meditation without an object comes after the separation between the meditator and the object of focus dissolves. When there is no longer a sense of someone meditating on something, and one enters a state of referencelessness, that is meditation without an object. Simply being can also be meditation without an object, or it could be remaining undistracted in the present moment, which is a subtle object. It depends on the experience of the meditator. Beginning with an object can lead to meditation free of any sense of object, subject and action, but it also may not, depending on how obscured the meditator's mind is. Either way, meditating on something is the way to begin and return to if you can't manage to just be, as described in the previous chapter.

A common object for meditation is the breath. That's what we'll be using as our object today, but the methods I teach here can also be used with any object, and in future chapters I'll introduce you to other objects that can be used as the focus of your meditation. Each has a different flavour, and people find some work better for them than others, so try them all. If you find one method that particularly inspires a calm, clear mind state, then use that for your practice.

The beauty of the breath is that it is always with us, so we can focus on it anytime. Also, breathing in and out consciously is a tool we often use automatically and effectively to help us handle emotions and pain. The reason for that is the relationship between the breath and the winds in our subtle channels (prana, or lung in Tibetan) but I won't go into that here; you can research it for yourself if you're interested. For our purposes, just know that a calm breath is related to a calm mind, so if you can calm your breathing when you're upset, it will help you calm your mind and vice versa.

So let's try the first of these meditation techniques.

Guided meditation
Sit in meditation posture with an upright spine, relaxed limbs, mouth slightly open and gaze relaxed.

Breathe in and out once in preparation and then allow yourself to breath normally and naturally.

Set an altruistic motivation for your meditation session. This will bring inspiration, power and greater focus to your practice. Say something like "May this meditation session bring benefit to all beings. May they be happy and free of suffering."

Now focus on your breathing.

Breathe in and breathe out as you normally do, and simply notice that that's what you're doing.

Don't focus 100% on your breathing. That kind of solid concentration can lead one to become heavy and fixated, even dull, whereas the true meditative state is much more relaxed and open.

So to assist our mind to find this open, clear and calm state, put only 25% of your focus on the object of meditation—in this case, your breath. Put another 25% of your focus on the part of your mind that is aware that you're meditating and pulls your focus back when it drifts off—that's your awareness—and leave the other 50% simply abiding spaciously.

You could focus on the feeling of the air going in and out through your nose.

Or you could focus on your chest rising and falling.

Simply be aware of your breath going in and out, steady and natural.

If your mind wanders away and starts thinking, just bring your attention back to your breathing.

Don't comment on it in any way, no chastisement, no commentary, don't even think, "Now I'm breathing out. Now I'm breathing in."

25% mindful of your breathing.

25% aware of your mind, making sure you stay focused on your breathing.

And 50% left relaxed, open and spacious.

This light touch can make a huge difference to the quality of your meditation.

Continue focusing on your breath and apply this recipe for how to hold your mind.

When thoughts arise, simply bring your focus back to the breath.

Repeat this again and again without commentary.

Don't aim to do anything more than this.

Let the thoughts come and go as they will. All you have to do is not get caught up in them.

If the sense of you meditating on anything starts to dissolve, great, let go of the object and rest in Shamata meditation without the support of an object (i.e., your breath). Simply remain undistracted from that clear open state.

When you lose it, that's the time to return to focusing on your breath again.

Simply breathe.

So you can go from meditation with an object to without an object and back again as it occurs naturally. This will make your mind very flexible.

Simply be.

Simply breathe.

Try pausing at the end of your out-breath, and as you breathe in, leave your mind in the gap between the out and the in-breaths. This can be a very powerful way to enter a deep state of meditation.

Enter the gap.

Now drop the technique and simply rest.

Just be.

As you are.

At the end of your session, once again make the aspiration that your meditation brings benefit to others as well as yourself.

Think something like 'May the benefit of this practice be shared with all beings, so they may be free of negative emotions and gain the ultimate happiness of enlightenment.'

Simply Seeing

Before you start, choose an object on which to focus—a flower, a crystal, a candle, a photo of an inspiring scene, or perhaps you have a nice view in your garden, or you can sit and look at the ocean. If you're a Christian, you might like to choose an inspiring picture of Jesus or the Virgin Mary or a saint, and, of course, you could use an image of the Buddha—whatever inspires your mind to peace and clarity.

Place your object somewhere you can see it without having to bend your neck and settle yourself in your chair or on your meditation cushion.

Begin by assuming the meditation posture. Keep your spine straight, legs crossed if you're on a cushion, or uncrossed and feet flat on the floor if you're on a chair. And keep your eyes open, at least partially.

You can start with them closed if you wish, but once your mind has settled, open them a little.

Have your hands resting on your knees, palms down, or in your lap, palms up, one hand on top of the other.

Tilt your chin down slightly, put your shoulders back, and have your mouth slightly open, as if you're about to say 'Ah.'

Take a deep breath in, and as you breathe out, drop your mind, like a pebble being thrown into a pool.

Then allow yourself to simply be.

Once your ordinary mind returns—be it after a nanosecond or several minutes—make the aspiration that your meditation practice will bring benefit to all sentient beings. Think: 'May this practice help all beings be happy and free from suffering.'

Then focus lightly on the object before you.

Make your gaze soft. Relaxed. And vast like the ocean.

Just sit and simply see whatever you're looking at.

...

Don't think about what you see, simply look.

No mental commentary is needed.

The idea is to look purely without evaluating what you see.

...

If you find yourself thinking about the object—or anything else—as soon as you realise what you're doing, just bring your attention back to simply seeing.

Just look.

And be aware that you're looking.

…

When you drift off, don't comment on the fact that you drifted off, just return your attention to the object.

And simply see.

…

Remember the recipe for how to hold your mind in meditation that I introduced in the Simply Breathing chapter:

25% of your mind focuses on the object of meditation, 25% is aware that you're meditating, and 50% of your mind simply abides spaciously.

Simply look.

Simply see.

And when your mind wanders off, bring it back to simply looking.

That's it, just keep doing that.

...

Over and over.

...

Eventually, your mind will calm and clear.

Then let go of any idea of focusing on an object and simply remain in that clear and peaceful state.

If you lose it, return your attention to whatever you're looking at.

50% of your attention on the object and 50% just abiding spaciously.

...

When you're finished, before getting up and going about your day, remember all those sentient beings again and dedicate the positive results of this practice to their benefit. Think something like "May the merit created by this practice benefit all beings." You can also add specific wishes or prayers for individuals or the world. Doing this benefits you as much as them; it leaves you in a warm, magnanimous mind state.

Simply Listening

Having a focus for your meditation is the usual starting point and one to which you can return when you become distracted during meditation without a focus. Simply listening is a favourite of mine, because I find it a reliable way to enter the pervasive sense of awareness that leads to resting in the nature of mind.

Before you start, find a good spot where you won't be disturbed—this technique works very well in nature, and you can use it when listening to music.

Begin by assuming the meditation posture. Keep your spine straight, legs crossed if you're on a cushion, or uncrossed and feet flat on the floor if you're on a chair. And keep your eyes open, at least partially.

Have your hands resting on your knees, palms down, or in your lap, palms up, one hand on top of the other.

Tilt your chin down slightly, put your shoulders back, and have your mouth slightly open, as if you're about to say 'Ah.'

Now take a deep breath in, and exhale slowly, expelling any negativity with your out-breath.

Then breathe normally.

…

To inspire yourself and make your meditation more powerful, think of others, make the aspiration that your meditation bring benefit to all beings. Imagine that whatever peace and clarity you attain spreads out from you like ripples in the water, touching everyone you interact with, and then everyone they interact with and so on.

'May all beings have happiness and be free from suffering.'

Then listen.

…

You could start by listening to one thing. The birds chirping, your children chatting, your breath flowing in and out, or some music playing quietly.

Don't think about the sound.

Don't even label it.

Don't get caught up in it.

Simply listen.

Hear what is to be heard without commentary.

…

If you find your mind wandering off into thoughts, then bring your attention back to the sound on which you're focusing.

…

If a jet passes overhead, or a car passes on the road outside, listen to that as it comes and passes away.

All these sounds will eventually fade, and when they do, follow the silence.

…

Now expand your listening—and your mind—to encompass everything you hear.

Don't focus on anything in particular.

Simply listen.

Without commentary.

Be aware that you're listening.

…

Of course, thoughts will come. Just as you can't have tea without leaves, you can't have meditation without thoughts. They are a natural expression of the nature of your mind.

We are not trying to get rid of them.

We just allow them to come and allow them to go without grasping onto them.

…

Allow your thoughts to pass through your mind without disturbing it.

…

The trick is not to hold onto your thoughts.

Just let them go.

And simply listen.

…

Hear what is to be heard.

No matter what it is: pleasant or unpleasant, treat both sounds the same.

Make no value judgement.

Simply listen.

To everything.

…

Allow your awareness to expand to encompass everything.

In all directions.

And remain there, undistracted from that awareness.

Simply be.

…

If you find yourself distracted, then return to listening to everything around you without focusing on anything in particular.

Simply listen.

Once you are undistracted again, drop the meditation.

And simply be.

…

When you've finished, remember to dedicate the benefit you gained from your meditation to the benefit of all beings. May it help them find peace, clarity and compassion.

Simply Watching

Thoughts are not your enemy
It's easy in meditation to get the idea that thoughts are our enemy, especially if we subscribe to the idea that the aim of meditation is to get rid of thoughts. As I explained in the chapter on 'What is Meditation?' thoughts slowing down and dissolving are a by-product of meditation, not the point of it. The point of meditation is to discover the true nature of our mind, the state where we are naturally clear and peaceful. That's where true inner peace meditation is found.

Why thoughts can be a problem
The method we use to help us experience this state is that of focusing on an object without distraction. Yes, our thoughts tend to distract us, but that doesn't mean they're bad, or that we should try to get rid of them. They are, after all, a natural expression of our mind, and as such can't be eradicated completely anyway. The problem is not having thoughts, it's that we tend to follow the thoughts; we get caught up in them; we think about them. We grasp onto them and allow them to distract and disturb us.

The solution: working with thoughts in meditation

So what we need to work on in meditation is our relationship to our thoughts. We need to loosen up that relationship.

A thought is no problem; the problem comes when we start a train of thoughts that follow it and get so caught up in the thought train that we lose ourselves.

Someone who has integrated meditation into their lives can see thoughts and emotions arising in their mind and not be perturbed by them. No matter what the content of the thought or emotion, they see it as just a thought or just an emotion, something that has no solid reality, and that is fleeting and unreliable.

They are aware of their thoughts and emotions and allow them to come and go naturally without getting involved with them. This makes them very peaceful, aware and loving people.

This ability comes as a natural by-product of practising meditation with any object, but we can practice it directly, and thus speed up the process, by using our mind as the focus of our meditation, just as we used our breath, or a visual object or a sound.

If we watch thoughts as the object of our meditation, they are no longer a distraction, they are simply what we're focusing on or, with a more spacious approach, what we're aware of.

The meditation technique for watching your mind

When we focus on our breath, or a visual or aural object, as soon as we notice that we've followed our thoughts somewhere else, we bring our mind back to our object of focus. It's the same here.

What we're watching is our thoughts coming and going; we're training ourselves not to engage with them, but to simply notice them as they pass through our mind—like clouds appearing out of and dissolving back into the sky. Just as we don't comment on the flower we're focusing on; we don't comment on or make thought trains about what we see in our mind.

I find it very helpful to think of my mind as like a movie screen and my thoughts as credits rolling in one side and out the other.

Try it.

Now.

Guided meditation

Begin by checking your meditation posture.

Sit with your spine straight and legs crossed, or if you're on a chair, put your feet flat on the floor.

Have your eyes half open and your hands palms down, resting on your knees, or in your lap, palms up, one hand on top of the other.

Tilt your chin down slightly, put your shoulders back, and have your mouth slightly open, as if you're about to say 'Ah.'

Now take a deep breath in, and exhale slowly, expelling any negativity with your out-breath.

Then breathe normally.

…

To frame our meditation in the most powerful way, think: 'May this practice help all beings be happy and free from suffering.'

Generate love and compassion for all beings without exemption.

…

Now let those thoughts go and consider your mind as like an empty movie screen.

If you find it helpful, you could visualise an empty screen in front of you, or just turn your attention onto your own mind.

Watch it as you would a blank movie screen, as if waiting for the movie to start.

...

Focus on that empty screen in a spacious, easy way.

...

When a thought comes, see it as a credit rolling in one side of the screen and out the other.

Don't follow the thought or think about the thought, just watch it roll across the screen of your mind.

...

Keep half your attention on the empty screen and the other half just relaxed and spacious.

Watch your thoughts come and go.

Without getting caught up in them.

...

If you find your mind wandering off, thinking about a thought, bring your attention back to the empty screen of your mind, here in the present moment.

Watch your mind and wait for the next thought to appear and float through.

...

If you have lots of thoughts all piling on top of each other, you may find it helpful to label them.

For example: if you think about the chocolate cake in the cupboard, you'd label that thought 'chocolate cake', then you'd let it go.

You could even smile and wave goodbye.

…

Approach the practice with an easy compassionate attitude towards your thoughts.

Whatever rises is fine.

It's just a thought.

Leave it alone and it'll pass through.

…

Don't try to stop your thoughts.

Just watch them as they roll onto that empty screen from one side, pass through, and then roll off the other side.

…

Or you could see them as rising from the empty screen of your mind, then dissolving back into it.

…

When your thoughts slow down, you'll find space between them.

Go into that space.

And remain there.

That's the nature of your mind: clear, fresh, open and awake, with love and compassion at its core.

…

When thoughts rise in this empty screen of your mind, see them, but let them be.

Let them fade in and out without bothering you, no matter what their content.

They are merely thoughts, just a natural expression of the nature of your mind.

…

Simply watch your mind.

And see the thoughts that pass through it.

…

If you find that you've got caught up in your thoughts, the moment you realise, look directly at the thought in your mind.

Hit it with your awareness.

Look straight at it.

Then look for the next thought.

See if you can catch one rising.

…

Sometimes when you do that, you find nothing there, no thoughts, just your own awareness, searching, waiting, ready and alert.

The very act of looking for thoughts can make them shy, and you can find yourself looking directly into the nature of your mind.

You'll know if that's so, because everything drops away. Your mind expands, becomes endless, unobstructed and filled with enormous clarity and a readiness to respond with compassion to whatever arises. The world becomes more vibrant, as if a veil has fallen from your perception.

…

Simply watch your mind.

…

At the end, remember all those sentient beings again and dedicate the positive results of your practice for their benefit.

Think: 'May the benefit of this practice be shared with all beings, so they may be free of negative emotions and gain the ultimate happiness of enlightenment.'

Integration: watch your mind

Watching your mind is a very powerful integration practice. It can be simply being aware of what you're thinking, or it can be being aware of the nature of your mind.

Just stop—anywhere, anytime—and turn your attention in to see what you're thinking.

Look for your thoughts.

See if you can catch one rising.

Simply Walking

There are several approaches you can take to walking meditation, so choose which approach best suits where you are on any day. Walking meditation is good because we walk throughout the day, so if we meditate every time we walk, then we are integrating meditation into our life in a very active way.

Walking meditation is also important if we're doing long meditation sessions. Our bodies need to move for us to stay alert, so it's a good way to perk up our meditation if it gets dull. Breaking up long periods of sitting with periods of walking is better for both body and mind than long periods of sitting without intervals of movement. It's also good integration practice.

The mindfulness approach to walking meditation

The mindfulness approach to walking meditation is a simple process of being mindful of your body. You put your attention on your body, and when you find yourself mentally wandering off after thoughts, you bring your mind back to your body.

You can focus on such things as your feet touching the ground, your arms cutting through the air, the weight of your body on the ground, the transfer of weight from one foot to another or simply the whole physical experience of walking. Simply be mindful and aware of your body as you walk and keep your focus on that.

To make this meditation an awareness meditation rather than just a mindfulness meditation, use the 25% mindful, 25% aware and 50% spacious recipe. 25% of your mind is focused on the physical feeling of your body walking, another 25% of your mind is aware that you're being mindful and when your mind wanders off, it brings it back to its point of focus, and half of your mind is simply being spacious. This means that your mind is open and light, not heavily fixated on the object of meditation—your walking.

The mantra approach

Sometimes we need something more to anchor our mind, and a mantra is excellent for that purpose. Mantras are also excellent for calming emotions and energising the body. You can use any of the mantras I talked about in the section on chanting meditation, use a short prayer if you're Christian, or even make up your own—just make sure that whatever you're saying over and over again is positive and helpful. You don't need to say it out loud, you can just think it, over and over, though saying it just enough that your lips move is good because you then use your breath, and that has beneficial effects on your body. Repeating a mantra will create a rhythm that will naturally find a way to compliment the rhythm of your walking. On Ah Hung works well for that.

When we use a mantra while we walk, we simply walk, being mindful of our body walking as before, but we add a mantra as further protection against our mind rushing elsewhere. It's hard to think about things when you're saying a mantra over and over.

The simply being approach

This is the same as simply being meditation, only you're walking while you do it. You're just resting in the present moment. You're aware that you're walking—you're aware of everything—and you're not distracted from the present moment, from simply being here now. This is easy to say and not so easy to do. For those with no or little experience in meditation, I suggest sitting for a moment first before trying this kind of open walking meditation. The idea is that you establish your sense of 'simply being' while sitting, then just maintain it as you walk.

Guided practice

When doing walking meditation formally, it's good to sit for a moment before you start and set a powerful motivation for the practice. So …

Let's begin.

Sit for a moment, making sure that your spine is straight to help clear the subtle channels and prepare you for walking with a good posture.

Think: 'May this practice help all beings be happy and free from suffering.' Take a moment to send this intention out into the universe.

...

Then stand and, keeping that nice straight spine, begin walking.

Be aware of your body as it moves through space.

...

Make sure that you aren't stooped, that you're walking tall with your shoulder back and head not thrust forward—but don't strain. Do it in a relaxed way.

Feel your spine running up the back of your body and your neck as its natural extension.

...

Fell your arms moving naturally. You might be able to feel the air on your skin as you walk.

...

Feel your feet pressing on the ground, and your weight transferring from one leg to the other.

….

Feel your whole body moving and simply walk.

…

Remain focused on the feeling of your body walking.

But keep your attention light with just half your mind focused on your body and the other half open, spacious and aware.

…

If your mind wanders off after thoughts, or if emotion carries you away, as soon as you realise, bring your attention back to the feeling of your body simply walking.

….

You could imagine that you're walking on lotus blossoms.

…

Or you could imagine that you're leaving a trail of lotus blossoms behind you in your footsteps.

…

You could imagine that you're walking towards an enlightened being, whichever one inspires you and you feel a connection with. Imagine them glowing with light.

…

When your mind wanders off, just bring your attention back to your walking.

...

If you find yourself in an undistracted state, then drop the meditation and simply walk.

...

When thoughts come, just let them rise and fall naturally, like waves in the ocean.

Don't cling to them or try to stop them.

Just let them fade away of their own accord.

Simply walk.

...

Be spacious with your focus. Keep it light so your awareness can blossom.

Be aware of everything around you.

But don't be distracted by whatever you see or hear.

Simply walk.

....

When thoughts come, simply bring your attention back to the feel of your body walking, or you could add a mantra and focus on that.

Just let those thoughts dissolve back into the space from which they arose.

…

Now drop the meditation and simply walk

without focusing on anything in particular

and without being distracted from you

simply walking,

here,

now.

…

Simply be

Walking.

…

If you lose that sense of simply being, go back to focusing on your body walking, or saying a mantra or short prayer as you walk.

Walk tall, relaxed and easy.

…

Alternate between meditating with a focus and meditating without a focus.

Simply walk.

...

When you've finished your walk, sit again for a moment and dedicate the benefit of your walking meditation to all beings.

'May the benefit of this practice be shared with all beings, so they may be free of negative emotions and gain the ultimate happiness of enlightenment.'

Practice every time you walk

The very fact that you walk throughout the day makes it an excellent tool for integrating your meditation practice into your life. How often do you get up from your desk at work, walk to the photocopier, do your copying and walk back to your desk with no mindfulness and awareness? Instead, make a commitment to walk mindfully, every step you take. Of course, it's good to set aside walking meditation practice sessions as well, but you can start right now, when you get up from reading this, just be mindful of your body walking. How does it feel as you move through space, as your feet touch the floor, step after step?

Whether you're doing a set walking meditation session or taking a few steps away from your desk, choose whichever method you feel is most beneficial for you at any time.

After you've become familiar with walking meditation in all its forms, you won't have to think about it, you'll just slip into the walking meditation mind state as soon as you take a step. It's all just a matter of training your mind.

Simply Mantra

In chanting meditation, the focus, of course, is on the chant. The object of the meditation here is an action. You focus on the act of chanting and the words of the chant. This is excellent practice for integrating meditation into daily life where you can replace the act of chanting as your focus with any act, for example, the act of washing dishes. When your mind wanders off from the act of chanting, you return your focus to the chant. You don't have to say the mantra out loud. You can just think it over and over in your mind.

Mantra and emotions

Meditation with a chant has another special benefit: it's very good for your energy. The sound, especially when it's a sacred syllable, resonates through the cells of your body and heals and lifts your spirits.

If you're trying to meditate but find yourself just too upset to settle, then try using a mantra and chanting it internally or vocally. You can feel emotions in your body, can't you? That's because emotions are energy in motion—e-motion. Sound vibrations move in the same subtle channels in the body, so making the right kinds of sounds can calm those wild emotions.

How do you feel when you sing a song—when no one else is around to care if you sound good or not? I always feel pretty good, and I figure most other people enjoy using their voices in that way. Happy songs make us happy, and sad songs make us sad; in the same way, songs that call forth your deepest nature do exactly that.

A mantra repeated over and over has enormous power, and just as different songs have different moods and effects on us, different mantras have different purposes beyond simply lifting our spirits or being a focus for meditation practice.

Your mantra could be an affirmation, like 'I am well' or 'all is well' or 'I am loved,' or anything else you want to say to yourself over and over. These can be good for alleviating anxiety, and you can change the affirmation mantra to suit your needs for a particular day or time in your life.

Personally, however, English affirmations as a mantra don't work well for me. My mind says things like 'No everything isn't well; there's a war in Ukraine; people are starving in Africa; there's an earthquake in Turkey,' and so on. I prefer the traditional Sanskrit chants with their esoteric meaning. You could also choose something in Latin, perhaps *Memento Vivere* (remember to live). You could alternate it with *Memento Mori* (remember death) which reminds you to live because death will come for us all.

A Sanskrit mantra - Om Ah Hung

The simplest mantra to chant is Om by itself. The next most simple is Om Ah Hung. But don't let simplicity fool you into thinking it's a starter kit only. Om Ah Hung is a powerful mantra at all levels of meditation practice.

Om is the open, endless, all-encompassing, unformed source of everything, the ineffable state from which everything springs. It is the sound of the essence of the universe and all creation itself. Its vibration alone calms the nervous system, and when you chant it, you bring yourself into alignment with the true nature of the universe. Reciting Om is a very powerful tool for bringing you peace and clarity and opening your mind to its deepest nature.

Ah is the expression of joy and wonder at the rich display of the wealth of phenomena coming into existence from out of the formless state of Om. It invokes the brilliant clarity of awareness and speaks of the endless possibilities of creativity.

Hung is the world of phenomena, the manifestation of the combination of formlessness (Om) and creativity (Ah). It is here and now and all its potential.

By chanting Om Ah Hung, you are invoking the power of the process of manifestation—drawn from the formless realm, pregnant with all possibility, propelled by the brilliant light of inspiration out and into manifestation as form. It's the very essence of magic!

If you don't want to actually vocalise the mantra, then just say it over and over in your mind. If, however, you'd like the energetic benefits of vocalising, then you could listen to a recorded chant (you can find many on YouTube), become familiar with it, then chant it yourself, while immersing yourself in the sound and the mind state it evokes.

Or simply take a deep breath and say Om, while letting your breath out slowly.

Allow your mind to open as the sound fades into nothing.

Be mindful of what you're doing but be very spacious about it. Allow your mind to soar.

Give yourself over to the sound.

Feel it vibrate through you.

Allow the power of the sacred syllable to open your mind to its vastest reaches.

Chant for as long or as short as you wish. Even one Om is good for you.

Now do the same for Ah, and then for Hung.

Then put the three syllables together.

Om Ah Hung

You can just say it quietly to yourself.

Slowly at first.

Let each sound ring out like a bell.

You can even say it fast, over and over, so it becomes like the sound of a bubbling river, the background to the flow of your meditation.

You can get a mala (Buddhist rosary) and count the mantras (use your left hand, flick each bead over with your thumb), not for the sake of numbers, but to give you an added action to help anchor your meditation. Aiming to do a certain number of mantras each day is also a good way to inspire you to do a certain length of practice. It helps you to be disciplined. The action of the fingers is also a method for helping to regulate your emotions, having the same effect as stimming does for an autistic person.

Guided mantra meditation

I have used Om Ah Hung as the mantra, but you can use 'I am well' or 'All is well' or any other words with meaning for you. Three words works well.

Begin by assuming the meditation posture. Keep your spine straight, legs crossed if you're on a cushion, or uncrossed and feet flat on the floor if you're on a chair. And keep your eyes open, at least partially.

You can start with them closed if you wish, but once your mind has settled, open them a little.

Have your hands resting on your knees, palms down, or in your lap, palms up, one hand on top of the other.

Tilt your chin down slightly, put your shoulders back, and have your mouth slightly open, as if you're about to say 'Ah.'

Now take a deep breath in, and exhale slowly, expelling any negativity with your out-breath.

Then breathe normally.

Open your heart and mind with a heartfelt wish that your practice benefit all sentient beings. Think: 'May this practice help all beings be happy and free from suffering.'

Take a deep breath and, as you breathe out, say 'Om' with a long sound.

Repeat it several times quietly.

... *Om, Om, Om* ...

When you feel comfortable with the sound, increase the volume.

... *Om, Om, Om* ...

You can play with the sound, use different tunes, or just keep it simple, whatever you're comfortable with. You can even just say it quietly to yourself.

However you chant it, allow your mind to soar with the chant.

… *Om, Om, Om* …

Give yourself over to the sound. Feel it vibrate through you.

… *Om, Om, Om* …

Allow the power of the sacred syllable to open your mind to its vastest reaches.

… *Om, Om, Om* …

Now, take a deep breath and say 'Ah', while letting your breath out slowly.

Allow your mind to open as the sound fades into nothing.

Repeat 'Ah' several times in the same way you did with Om.

… Ah, Ah, Ah …

… Ah, Ah, Ah …

Now move on to 'Hung'. Say it the same way as you did for 'Om' and 'Ah', making the sound long.

… Hung, Hung, Hung …

… Hung, Hung, Hung …

Now put the three syllables together:

… Om Ah Hung …

Slowly at first.

… Om, Ah, Hung …

Let each sound ring out like a bell.

… Om, Ah, Hung …

Then increase the speed and volume.

… Om, Ah, Hung …

Try saying it fast, over and over, so it becomes like the sound of a bubbling river, the background to the flow of your meditation.

… Om, Ah, Hung …

Try a melody. Play with the sounds.

… Om, Ah, Hung …

At the end of the meditation, let the chant drop and remain simply being in silence.

Simply Imagining

This meditation uses an imagined visual image as the object of focus. We visualise a representation of the essential nature of awakened mind—open, endless, aware, compassionate, and all encompassing, the very nature of reality itself.

And we are not separate from this essential nature. It is the true nature of our own mind and of all phenomena. So what we choose as our visual image also must represent our awakened mind, our wisest, most loving and aware, essential self. It needs to be an image we can relate to as this deepest aspect of ourself. This is why it's best to use a human figure. The Tibetans call them deities. I call them noble beings. But whatever you call them, these meditational supports are essentially representations of aspects of our own awareness.

Finding your noble being

Before you start the meditation, take some time to find an image of your noble being that you can see in your mind. You can make it very simple; a shining being made of light, neither male nor female, without adornment, but containing all the love, compassion, wisdom and power of the universe. Or you can go for something more detailed, a form that represents your most vibrant noble self.

Sit quietly, allow your mind to settle and set the intention of seeing your noble self in your mind's eye. Allow your mind freedom to create something uniquely for you at this time in your life. (Noble beings can appear in many different forms, so it's not a 'create an image and stick with it for life' kind of thing.)

You may imagine a queen or kingly figure, a goddess or god, a high priestess, a sage, a mage, whatever inspires you. Whatever its form, your noble self is best visualised in a form that inspires you, as someone young, healthy, beautiful, wise and fearless. As your noble self you wear flowing silken robes and are adorned with symbols of love, compassion, wisdom and awareness in the form of hair adornments, necklaces, rings, bracelets and so on. Or the noble being can be free of all adornments.

The most important thing is that your noble being, your representation of your essential wisdom self is made of rainbow light. They are not solid, not flesh and blood, but the clear light of awareness.

Guided imaginative meditation

First, settle into your meditation posture and set the intention that the meditation help you bring benefit to all beings.

Visualise your mind as a blue sky, open, endless, and crystal clear.

Take a moment to stabilise this image and rest your mind in its vast openness.

Then gather all the endless wisdom, compassion and spiritual power of the universe, including your own, and visualise it as a star sparkling in the vast sky.

The star grows and coalesces into the form of a noble being made of light. Visualise a regal figure, young, healthy, beautiful, wise and fearless. They wear flowing silken robes and are adorned with symbols of love, compassion, wisdom and awareness in the form of exquisite hair adornments, glistening necklaces and anklets, and rings and bracelets set with precious stones. Your noble being is not solid, but made of light, of the clear light of awareness.

This noble being is your wisest, most aware and loving self, the essential nature of your mind and of reality itself. Take time to visualise them clearly, bringing your mind back to the visualisation if it wanders off.

Then imagine brilliant loving awareness shining forth from their heart centre and pouring into you, filling you with endless love, dissolving all your worries and boosting your health.

Here you can recite a mantra if you wish. Repeat it, in your mind or out loud, as many times as you wish as you visualise the light pouring into you. Something like, 'I am loved' or 'All is well,' or 'Om Ah Hung', or even 'I take refuge in endless, open, loving awareness.'

Feel your heart warm.

Know you are lovable, and you are loved.

Rest in that endless flow of loving light until you are so filled with love that you are love itself, then imagine yourself flying up into the noble being and merging yourself with them. Visualise yourself as the noble being, made of light, adorned with the jewels of awareness, floating in space. Your mind is their mind, the mind of all awakened beings throughout time. It is wide open, endless, brilliantly aware, unfailingly compassionate, and all encompassing. Rest in that state of unity.

When you feel moved to action. Send your loving light out from your heart centre into the universe in all directions, sending love to all beings everywhere. The universe sends its light back into you, creating an endless nurturing circle. Rest there in perfect balance. Loving light coming in. Loving light going out.

When it's time to end the meditation, dissolve yourself from the outside of yourself into your heart centre, and then into nothing. Rest your mind in the space that remains and experience the calm clarity of your pure awareness.

When thoughts return, end the meditation by offering the benefit you received to all beings.

Simply Healing

The benefits of visualisation

The benefits of visualisation for healing are becoming more widely accepted. As I mentioned earlier, scientific studies have shown that basic meditation lowers blood pressure, improves immune systems and has other health benefits. A meditation session can leave you feeling so refreshed that it's as if you can feel your cells humming with health and vitality.

When visualisation is combined with meditation, the effect is particularly powerful; add spiritual chants whose sounds energise the body and clear the subtle channels and you have an even more potent recipe for healing. Vajrayana Buddhism also has mantras and visualisation specifically for healing, and when done after receiving the appropriate instruction from a master, they have enormous healing power.

How this meditation works
Today I'll give you a simplified version of such a meditation. One that can be done by anyone. How effective it will be will depend on how able you are to connect with your true nature, so the more meditation you've done, the better.

This meditation works by recognising that on one level, you are already healed. That there is a 'you' that is always well, always happy, always good. Buddhists call this Buddha Nature; for Christians, it's the holy spirit or Christ consciousness, but whatever you call it, this 'self', which is beyond 'self', beyond ideas of you and others, is your natural state, and your health issues, your stress and your dis-ease, is all a result of your ego-self, the false self, the one we believe we are, but is actually just a construction of convenience. If we saw our ego-self for what it is—a collection of multiple elements that is not permanent and doesn't exist independently from anything else—it would not be a problem, but when we identify with our ego-self, troubles arise, and all illness is ultimately the result of this misidentification.

You are not your illness
I'm going to repeat the image I used in the introduction because it's particularly useful here:

> Imagine a diamond, pure, clear and sparkling, covered by a layer of mud. No matter how much

mud accumulates around that diamond, the diamond itself is never stained by the mud. It can always be washed off because the mud is not part of the nature of the diamond. Your true nature is the diamond, but you don't see that because it's covered in mud. You see the mud and think that's who you are.

It's easy to identify with your sickness and forget that it is not who you are. You may have a sickness or disease, but you are not the disease. It's important to understand this, because you can become so focused on your health issues that you can lose sight of yourself as a person separate to your issues. This meditation will help you get in touch with your healthy self, your true nature where physical healing has the best chance of occurring.

Guided Practice: A simple but powerful healing meditation

So settle yourself into a meditation posture, with your spine erect and shoulders back leaving a gap between your elbows and your body. Legs crossed, or if you're on a chair, place them flat on the floor. You can also do this meditation lying on your back or propped up in bed with cushions behind you.

Rest your hands on your knees or in your lap in a relaxed and easy way. Take a deep breath in and release it out through your mouth. Then breathe normally.

To expand the power and effectiveness of this practice, wish that all beings without exemption will receive the same benefit from this practice as you. Think: 'May this practice help all beings be happy and free from suffering.'

The object of focus for this meditation is a visualisation. You can close your eyes if you need to.

Visualise that above your head is a pure white light, an embodiment of all the healing power of the universe and the stainless purity of the nature of your mind.

Get a strong sense of the power, compassion and presence of this light. Accept that it has the power to heal your body.

Once you have a clear sense of the presence of this brilliant light, visualise healing nectar in the form of liquid light pouring down from the embodiment of the healing power of the universe and into you.

Chant Om Ah Hung aloud a few times (if you feel you can), and then say it quietly to yourself, or simply think it. And as you chant, imagine the luminous light dripping through you and into the ground below, washing away all your illness.

Om Ah Hung

Om Ah Hung

Om Ah Hung

The liquid light flushes away diseased cells, harmful bacteria and viruses. It kills cancer cells, heals broken bones, burns, and any other problem you may have.

Om Ah Hung

Om Ah Hung

Om Ah Hung

Your illnesses and negative karma flow out of you in the form of black soot, smoke and tar, and disappear into the ground below you.

Om Ah Hung

Om Ah Hung

Om Ah Hung

The luminous healing nectar also washes away your negative emotions, negative karma and everything that obscures your true nature.

Om Ah Hung

Om Ah Hung

Om Ah Hung

Keep chanting and imagining your illnesses being flushed from your body until you feel you have removed all illness, negative emotions, negative karma and obscurations.

Then visualise yourself as completely clear, like a crystal vase.

Om Ah Hung

Om Ah Hung

Om Ah Hung

The healing nectar continues to flow and now fills you with energy and restores your immune system. It also clears your subtle channels so that your energy flows well on all levels.

Om Ah Hung

Om Ah Hung

Om Ah Hung

You become like a crystal vase filled with luminous milk.

Then the brilliant white light melts into you. See yourself shining brilliant white, and know that you are completely healed and purified.

Om Ah Hung

Om Ah Hung

Om Ah Hung

Then send that healing light to others who are unwell, and then to every being in the universe.

Om Ah Hung

Om Ah Hung

Om Ah Hung

Be a fountain of healing energy for the world. Let it flow through you in an endless stream.

Om Ah Hung

Om Ah Hung

Om Ah Hung

When you've finished, dissolve yourself into a spec of light and then into nothing.

Allow your mind to rest in that space without any point of reference.

...

Simply be.

...

To seal your practice and increase its potency, make a wish that your practice brings benefit to all beings.

'May the benefit of this practice be shared with all beings, so they may be free of negative emotions and gain the ultimate happiness of enlightenment.'

Then just sit quietly for a few moments before going about your day.

Simply Loving

Loving Kindness meditation has a different kind of object on which to focus—the feeling of loving kindness expressed with the words: 'May you be happy; May you be well; May you be safe'.

Any time you think of others rather than just yourself, your mind and heart opens and loosens. This makes it easier for you to enter into deep meditation because to some extent you've already stepped outside of your ordinary, selfish mind. Loving kindness and compassion practices are a way of breaking the hold our ego has over our mind.

The word 'ego' in Buddhism means grasping at a false sense of self. It's the part of us that identifies with the mud over the diamond or the clouds obscuring the sky. It's the part of us that thinks we *are* the clouds—our thoughts and emotions—when really we're the sky—our true nature, open, clear and compassionate. The aim of meditation is to come to know our true self, and loving kindness and compassion practices help us to do that by breaking our identification with what isn't that true self.

Guided loving kindness Practice

Start by reminding yourself that doing this practice will not only help you, but because you'll become calmer and kinder, it will also help everyone else you come in contact with.

To strengthen this, think: 'May this practice make all sentient beings be well, happy and free from suffering.'

...

Sit with your back straight, shoulders relaxed and hands resting on your knees or your lap. It's best to stay upright, but you can close your eyes if you wish, and you can do it lying down if you're unwell.

...

Take a moment to find the strongest memory of love that you can.

Try to remember someone who has shown you love, but not your boyfriend or your girlfriend because that love may be mixed with lust. If you can't find a memory of feeling loved by someone else, then find a memory of you loving someone else. Even if it is just you feeling love for a pet, that's enough.

...

If you can't find a memory of love, then find a time when you felt happy and safe or simply how you felt when someone was kind to you.

Or you can imagine the unconditional love of an enlightened being filling you with love.

...

Allow the memory to arouse the happiness and love in you. Fill yourself with it ... completely immerse yourself in it.

...

Say to yourself, 'May I be happy; May I be well; May I be safe'.

Keep recalling how love and happiness feels and fill yourself with it. Flood yourself with brilliant white light or warm golden light.

...

Say 'May I be happy; May I be well; May I be safe', over and over again.

...

Really feel happy, well and safe.

...

Stay in that feeling, bask in it for a while, and when your heart feels full, send it back to the person who made you feel loved, or who you loved, or who helped you feel happy. Send it as white or golden light and say 'May you be happy; May you be well; May you be safe'.

...

Know for sure that your love makes them well and happy.

Imagine them feeling well and happy.

...

Then send your love out to others,

first to the person who made you feel loved,

...

then one by one to everyone in your family

...

and then to your friends.

...

Think, 'May you be happy; May you be well; May you be safe'.

...

Imagine that the light of your love fills each of them with happiness.

…

Now send it to others you come across in your life, people you see but don't really know, like people at work, or who serve you in shops or who you pass in the street.

Think, 'May you be happy; May you be well; May you be safe'.

…

Now send it to someone that you find a little difficult or who irritates you. Try not to close down, keep your heart open and consider the following.

Like you, they just want to be happy, but are they happy? Wish that they be happy. Send them white or golden light and say, 'May you be happy; May you be well; May you be safe'.

…

If you lose the feeling of warmth and openness in your heart, then return to the scene you used to make you feel loved and happy, and immerse yourself in that feeling again. Feel that you are happy, well and safe, then continue.

…

Send light to the person you have difficulty with.

Say 'May you be happy; May you be well; May you be safe' and imagine them feeling happy and strong inside.

If they felt happy and well, they would be a kinder person, so helping them this way helps you and anyone else they meet.

…

Now send your love and light to all the places in the world where people are suffering or are not happy. Think: 'May you be happy; May you be well; May you be safe' and imagine them all happy, well and safe.

…

Then send your love to everyone in the universe, including the animals and insects. Think: may they be happy, may they be well and imagine them all happy, well and safe.

…

Now just relax and stay in that space.

Just be in a vast open state of loving kindness.

…

If you find yourself wandering off after thoughts, just let them go and return to thinking, 'May you be happy; May you be well; May you be safe'.

When you've finished, think, 'May the merit I've gained from this practice help all beings conquer delusion and gain the ultimate happiness of enlightenment.'

This practice can also be done throughout the day. Whenever you see another person, think: 'May you be happy; may you be well'.

Simply Aware - Beyond a Focus

Shamata and Vipassyana

I wrote earlier about the two kinds of meditation, Shamata and Vipassyana: Shamata being meditation within the realm of the ordinary conceptual mind, where you focus on an object, and Vipassyana being the clear seeing or insight that comes from going beyond the ordinary conceptual mind. Apart from 'simply being', the techniques of meditation I've given so far have been Shamata, because they have an object—the breath, visual objects, aural objects, thoughts, chants, and visualisation—but all of these are jumping off points for going beyond the focus. Shamata stabilises the mind so that Vipassyana can naturally follow. There are ways we can encourage the dawning of Vipassyana, but if your mind is resting peacefully without distraction, it can open of its own accord, without you having to do anything.

Experiencing your true nature

Remember the first technique for meditation that I gave you? It was 'simply being'. Those instructions gave you no focus for your meditation; the words were to help you simply rest in your natural mind without effort. Sometimes when we simply be, our ordinary mind can drop away and our awareness can blossom into a brilliant panoramic awareness. It feels as if your head has expanded and everything sharpens and becomes more vibrant. Thoughts have disappeared, and if they rise, they're insignificant and don't remain, like tiny wisps of clouds in an otherwise clear sky. Your sense of self dissolves and you have a sense of being one with everything. When you experience your mind as endless openness, brilliant clarity and oneness with everything that includes a natural sense of compassion, you've likely gone beyond the conceptual mind. You've also experienced your true nature, and that's the real point of meditation.

Usually, we just get little glimpses of this first, and our task then is to return to that state as often as we can. The long-term aim is to be in that state every moment of the day and night.

Though it is quite simple in theory—we just drop our ordinary mind, then remain without altering anything—most of us will need some help to get to the point where our conceptual mind can release. We have to train ourselves to get to the point where we can do nothing.

The key is letting go

Just as we can follow the instructions for simply being and not enter this state, we can follow the instructions for focusing on an object like the breath and still find the object of our meditation dissolving along with our sense of our self as the meditator (subject), meditating on (action) something (object). The key to going beyond Shamata into Vipassyana, beyond the conceptual mind into the true nature or essence of mind, is letting go. We need to let go of our thoughts, our concepts, our beliefs, everything.

Ego is constantly engaged in defending, building or maintaining its image of who we are, so everything we experience is sorted into what it rejects, accepts or ignores as being useful for its purpose. To go beyond the ordinary mind, we need to drop all this activity and simply be as we are, without artifice, without grasping at anything. No evaluation of the objects of our perception. The idea is to let everything simply be as it is. If we can do this, then our grasping will dissolve and the clear insight of Vipassyana can begin to dawn.

This is a very deep letting go. And it feels great.

Ways to encourage going beyond.

Though our ordinary mind can fall away and reveal the true nature of our mind as a natural result of having a strong Shamata practice, that won't always happen, and for some people it won't happen at all, but there are ways to encourage that blossoming.

1. Sitting with someone who is resting in the essential nature of their mind

Someone who has realised the essential nature of their mind and can transmit that realisation to others provides a shortcut to experiencing your true nature. Someone residing in that state has a strong presence that can be felt by those around them. If you sit with an open and appreciative mind your mirror neurons will reflect the mind state of the person sitting in the essential nature of their mind and give you a taste of the nature of your own mind—which is not different to theirs. Mirror neurons are why we tend to smile when someone smiles at us; it's a natural response to reflect the behaviour of another.

2. Dissolving a visualisation

The point in a visualisation meditation where we dissolve the visualisation into nothingness is a very powerful way of helping us to go beyond the conceptual mind. As in the imaginative meditation where the instructions tell us to imagine ourselves dissolving from the outside in, until we're nothing but a speck of light at our heart which then disappears into nothing. We then allow our mind to rest in that space without any point of reference. Try remaining in that state of referencelessness without changing anything.

3. Shamata without object

At any point in any of the meditations, we can drop the object and simply rest undistracted without being focused on anything. It is, in fact, a very good thing to do because this is the relaxed peaceful mind state in which we want to live our lives.

All the meditations presented here have an instruction at some point for letting go of the meditation and just being, that's Shamata without an object. You let go of the sense of you meditating on something (or of reading something) and just rest without any focus.

If you haven't recognised the nature of your mind, you'll still be in your conceptual mind, with nowness as a subtle object of your meditation, but that's great, not only because it's a wonderful state to be in, but also because Shamata without an object is the best place to be for launching beyond the ordinary mind. It's the take-off point, and the next step is becoming aware of your awareness.

4. Turning awareness onto itself

Once you can simply rest undistracted without being focused on anything in particular (as in point 3), the next step is to become aware of your awareness.

The key instruction is to turn your awareness inwards to look at itself, and the first step in that is to become aware of your own awareness.

Look for that part of yourself that is aware that you are meditating, the part that brings your mind back when it wanders off distracted.

You could call it the watcher.

Look at the watcher.

What is it that is aware of that watcher?

Your awareness.

Look at your own awareness and ask yourself:

What is this awareness?

What is its colour? Shape? Size?

Where does it come from?

Where does it reside?

Where does it go to?

Can you even find it?

Or does it always slip away from your grasp?

And yet, aren't you aware that you can't find it?

…

This is a method for exploding the watcher, for going beyond the idea of a meditator meditating on something and contemplating on these questions will lead you towards a deeper experience of the nature of your awareness. For a full guide to this kind of examination, I recommend the book *Clarifying the Natural State*, by Dakpo Tashi Namgyal (Rangjung Yeshe Books, 2001).

Two things can happen here: You can see the awareness as a thing, an object of some kind, or just a nowness, in which case—though it's still an amazing mind state of openness and awareness—you remain within the realm of the conceptual mind, or you can see the true nature of the awareness, which has no 'thingness', and go beyond the conceptual mind.

If this process leads you to experience your mind as wide open, without boundary, empty of thoughts, and free of grasping, along with a referenceless compassion, you may be tasting what Buddhist call shunyata – empty of is-ness, or inexpressible openness.

This pristine awareness is the true nature of our mind. It is who we truly are, and discovering this and remaining undistracted from it is the whole point of meditation at its deepest level.

It can feel as if your skull explodes and your awareness becomes incredibly clear and panoramic, as if seeing everything at once. Or it can be very ordinary – but in my experience, that comes later after repeated experience.

No matter how you experience the essential nature of your mind – a mind shattering event or a gentle opening into an all-pervasive clarity of mind – the essence of our mind is empty, its nature is clarity, and its energy is that of compassion. These are just words though, not the experience itself. Don't get caught up in concepts about it.

Going beyond the conceptual mind is more likely to happen if you also have experience in numbers 1, 2 and 3 in this section. The more experience in those, the more likely you are to be able to break through the conceptual mind and experience the freedom beyond.

It's with us always but we don't recognise it.

I don't think it's hard for us to have a glimpse of this state of awareness, because it's with us always; what's difficult is recognising it, being able to say 'that's it'. In order to be able to return to this state at will and know we're in the right place, then we need to be able to recognise it. This is where a teacher who has not only experienced their true nature but is also able to share that experience with others is helpful.

Traditional Dzogchen and Mahamudra masters are trained to do this—I recommend Mingyur Rinpoche (who has excellent online courses)—and if you're introduced to the nature of your mind often enough, you'll eventually recognise it. In a small group, you may even have the opportunity to have your meditation checked by the teacher, and if not, a good teacher will give plenty of instructions as to how you can be sure you have actually 'got it'.

You don't need to be a Buddhist to get the benefit from sitting with one of these teachers, and these Dzogchen and Mahamudra teachings, the highest teachings in the Tibetan tradition, go beyond any religion and are relevant to all.

Guided practice – simply aware

This practice does not focus on any object, and, as such, is for those with enough experience of meditation to be able to rest undistracted in the present moment, for at least a short period of time.

If your mind is distracted, you need an object for your meditation. Meditation with the support of an object anchors your mind, but once you're undistracted, you just rest in present awareness.

So let's begin by checking our posture and establishing a vast motivation for our practice.

Sit with your spine straight and legs crossed, or if you're on a chair, feet flat on the floor.

Have your eyes half open and your hands palms down on your knees, or palms up in your lap, one hand on top of the other.

Tilt your chin down slightly, put your shoulders back, and have your mouth slightly open, as if you're about to say, 'Ah.'

Take a deep breath in, and exhale slowly, expelling any negativity with your out-breath.

…

Make your meditation truly powerful by taking a moment to wish that all beings without exemption receive the benefit of this practice.

…

Now simply drop your mind.

Like a pebble dropped into a pool of water.

Splash!

Let everything go,

And simply be,

Aware.

Don't focus on anything.

Just relax, and let everything be as it is.

Don't even try to relax.

And let go of the idea of letting go.

Don't try to be peaceful.

Drop even the idea of meditation.

Just rest in the present moment, aware of everything around you.

If you become distracted, either come back to the present moment, or if you need something more tangible, focus on your breath, or on listening, or looking until your mind settles again. Once you're undistracted, drop the meditation again and just rest in the moment.

Simply be.

Aware.

…

Don't cling to any thoughts that arise,

just let them go.

…

Thoughts and emotions are not you.

You are much bigger than them.

…

Feel your presence,

in the moment.

…

Become aware of your awareness—a natural clarity, openness and presence.

Remain in that, without altering anything.

…

Let even the notion of meditating dissolve.

…

Now look at your awareness.

…

Can you find it?

Does it have a shape?

Look.

Does it have a colour?

A form?

Can you see it?

Hear it?

Touch it?

…

Look for it.

Try to locate it.

…

Even if you can't find it, you're aware that you can't find it, aren't you?

Awareness is aware that it can't find itself.

Be aware of that awareness.

And simply remain.

Simply aware.

Undistracted.

…

When you've finished make a wish that your practice helps all beings to recognise their essential nature.

Establishing a Regular Practice

How often should we meditate?

A lot of people want to meditate. They know that it's a good thing to do; they may even have had some instruction—like this book—but that doesn't mean that they actually do practice. Many go to a weekly session of meditation, which is great, but they can't quite manage to get into the habit of meditating daily at home.

Is meditating daily important? It is if you want to get the full benefit of meditation. A weekly or occasional session is great, of course, much better than not doing it at all, but you'll feel the benefits faster and more powerfully if you meditate daily. You'll also find it easier to integrate meditation into your daily life.

How about three times a week? That's also great, but if you forget or life intrudes on your plans, you may find it quickly becoming only once a week. If we aim to meditate daily, then if we miss a day here or there, it won't matter so much. It's also easier to make a daily habit than different habits for different days of the week.

So I recommend that you aim for a daily meditation practice.

How long should a practice be?

This is a common question and one to which there isn't a definitive answer. A meditation practice session could be anywhere from a nanosecond to many years.

A nanosecond? Yes. Every time we turn our awareness inwards to look at our mind, that is meditation. It could be that we simply notice what we're thinking, or it could be that we have a glimpse of the nature of our mind. If we remain undistracted for the moment that we have the intention to pay attention to our mind, then we are meditating.

On the other end of the scale, you can enter a full meditation retreat where you are meditating every moment of the day and night with different practices for the day and the night. These can be anywhere from a few weeks to any number of years.

Twenty minutes is often cited as a good length, but fifteen minutes is also a good length and so is forty minutes. There is no length of meditation that is not a good length.

Few have the right circumstances or desire for long retreats, but we can all meditate for a nanosecond every day.

If we think we have to meditate for a set time, we may be setting up a situation where we feel we don't have that time. We want to meditate for twenty minutes, but only have ten, so we skip our practice. Wouldn't it be better to practise for just ten minutes, or five if that's all we can manage?

The best thing is not to get hung up on the time length, rather to simply take some time each day to turn our mind inwards and look into our own mind.

If we leave the time open, then a short time can easily become a long time. We just have to allow ourselves the space.

What is more important than the length of time is the time of day we set aside for our meditation practice. To make it a habit, we need to do it at the same time every day. If we don't set a time, it won't become part of our daily routine.

When should we meditate?

The very best time to meditate is first thing in the morning, before you go about your day, even before you wash your face or have your breakfast. Get up, go to the toilet then straight to practise.

If you have a family or share a house with others, wake up before everyone else. That way, you won't be disturbed and you won't get caught up in the morning activities of others. I did a lot of practice while my daughter was small, mostly between 5 and 7 a.m. in the morning. I loved having that time to myself. It was such a treat, and a lovely way to start the day. I had to go to bed early to achieve it, but I never felt I was missing out on anything. I was gaining so much more.

If you're a night person rather than a morning person, you may need to make your coffee first! But don't let yourself start thinking about the day ahead; instead, make your coffee-making a meditation in itself by focusing spaciously on your actions, and not following after your thoughts.

Once your mind has spiralled off into planning your day, you've stepped onto the busy bus, and it'll likely speed you through your day, your desire to meditate forgotten among your long list of things you want to achieve.

I always tell my student to fall out of bed and onto their cushion—or into their meditation chair. Alternatively, don't get up at all, just prop yourself up in bed, take a deep breath, turn your mind inward and simply be. If you find yourself unable to remain undistracted in the present moment, then use any of the other methods I've described here. Simply being in a relaxed and spacious way is an excellent way to begin, though.

Make a cosy spot

Make the place where you meditate very cosy, a place you like to go. Give yourself something inspiring to look at, light a candle, or some incense if you like—or do none of it. The important point is that the place where you meditate should be somewhere that draws you, a place you find pleasant and peaceful.

How to structure the practice

So you're up before anyone else in the house and you're sitting in your chair or on your cushion in your cosy mediation spot. Now what?

It's easier to maintain a practice if you have a structure of some kind, and the simplest structure is also the one that will make your practice the most powerful. I mentioned it in the chapter on motivation. It's framing your practice with wishes for the benefit of others and keeping a spacious attitude during the practice.

In summary:

- Start by making a wish that the power of your practice will free all beings from suffering.
- During the practice, aim not to get caught up in your conceptual mind. Take a vast spacious attitude to whatever rises. Let thoughts and emotions be nothing more than ephemeral clouds in the brilliant sky of your mind.

- At the end, dedicate the benefit of the practice to all beings. Think something like *May all beings realise the primordial state of awareness.*

No matter how short your practice is, if you frame it this way, it will have enormous power. No matter how long it is, if you don't frame it this way, its power will be limited. Why? Because your mind will be limited.

Other structures

The loving kindness and healing meditations I mentioned here are examples of practices with more complex structures, but they are still framed in the same way—spaciousness sandwiched between thoughts for the wellbeing of others.

A simple and excellent structure that leads our mind step by step deeper into meditation is to start with focusing on an image, follow it up with chanting a mantra and end by either watching the breath or simply being, or both. The silence at the end of a chant can be very evocative.

Something that works well for some people is to count mantras using a mala or Buddhist rosary of 108 beads. I used to aim to do the same amount every day, and achieving that number gave me a real sense of satisfaction. Without that impetus, I doubt I would have done the amount of formal practice that I did. Others, however, find that counting mantras is not right for them at all. You do what works best for you.

If you go further into Buddhism, you will find many other practices, for example the Vajrayana Preliminaries which combine visualisation, chanting and prayer, and they're great for anyone who gets bored with just sitting. These practices not only give us something to do while we're practising, but also the visualisations and mantras are powerful methods for getting rid of the mud that covers the diamond of our true nature.

Whether you choose a simple structure or a more complex one, the point here is that a structure gives you a sense that you have something to do and gives you a sense of satisfaction when you have completed that.

Plan your practice, but be flexible

Everything changes. Everything. All the time. So though you need to have a plan for your practice sessions—even if it's just that you'd like to sit for five minutes—be prepared to change that plan as circumstances change.

What you do for the next few months doesn't have to be what you do for the rest of your life. If at the end of five minutes you are in such a great space that you want to sit longer, then sit longer. If you don't have twenty minutes, then sit for however many minutes you do have. If you have a sore throat, then don't chant today, do the healing meditation instead and so on.

I have seen many students set out with detailed plans of what practice they will do, then throw it all away because they find they have less time than they thought they would. Instead of discarding the whole practice, they could just do less each day.

So have three lengths of practice worked out. The long one for when you have time or are really inspired, the mid-length one for every day, and the short one for when you sleep in.

Be kind to yourself and be clever

It's amazing how tricky our ordinary mind can be in avoiding practising. Students have been known—myself included—to have arguments with themselves trying to get themselves to the cushion. I have literally dragged myself kicking and screaming onto the cushion some days. Other days I have simply had a break. If we want to make meditation a part of our life, there's no point setting up a struggle within ourselves, we have to find skilful ways to let the struggle go.

Sometimes the skilful way is giving up for an hour or a day; sometimes it's not meditating but listening to an inspiring teaching or reading a book instead. Often once we have diffused the situation, the part of us that loves our meditation will come to the fore and we can then get on with our meditation.

Whatever happens, don't beat yourself up over it. Don't allow your desire to have a daily practice be a reason to feel disappointed in yourself if you don't manage it. Just note that you didn't manage it today and make the aspiration that you will do it tomorrow. Deal with yourself as you do your thoughts in meditation—with compassion and spaciousness.

Never give up

If you really want to meditate, if you recognise the benefits it will bring you, and if you understand that on the day you die, you will truly need the mental peace and stability that meditation brings, then you will eventually get a regular practice going. The important thing is to never give up.

I have seen students take ten years before they get a daily practice going, and the reason they finally get it together is simply that they never gave up wanting to.

Guided meditations

Another thing that will help you to get a practice going is my audio guided meditations. You can find them on Bandcamp. The album is called *Simply Being Guided Meditation*.
https://tahlianewland.bandcamp.com/album/simply-being-guided-meditation

These make it easy for you to remember the instructions and, as such, are an essential companion to this book.

Effortless effort

I used the word 'easily' in the title of this book and yet some discipline is required to establish a regular practice. However, our effort can be effortless effort. We can do what is required in a relaxed easy way, with the same mental posture that we use in meditation—50% focused on what we're doing and 50% spacious. And once we have the discipline, the practice will come easily. It will become such a cherished part of our life that we won't want to miss it.

Meditation is time for ourselves; it's a quiet, peaceful time that many of us don't get otherwise in our lives. And yet, we need it. It is, in fact, vital for mental, physical and spiritual health. We need not only the peace, but also the insight that comes from meditation, from taking time to look within. Meditation is the greatest gift we can give ourselves.

Being present is a present to ourselves, and to others, and when we take that presence into our daily life, it transforms our perception and our interactions with others in such a way that it can, indeed, transform our lives.

Integration: Stop Now and Meditate

The practice of meditation is the practice for the real practice which is life. Ultimately, meditation is not something we do for its own sake, we do it to transform our mind every moment of the day and night. When we sit still and focus on an object with the aim of experiencing our innate pure awareness, we are developing the mental skills and flexibility we need to engage with phenomena and life events in a sane way.

At the moment, most of us live our lives in a rather neurotic fashion. We believe every thought that appears in our mind; worse still, we believe we are those thoughts. When we feel happy, we think we are happy, and when we experience sadness, we think we are sadness itself. We identify with our thoughts and emotions so completely that we have no separation from them. We are completely caught up in them—slaves to our own minds.

This makes us very unhappy, and the only way to break this cycle of insanity is to learn meditation so that we gain the ability to step back from our thoughts and emotions, to shrug off their hold on us, and to see them as what they really are—merely thoughts, with no more reality than a mirage.

But if we only do this when on the meditation cushion, the benefit will be limited. At the moment of our death we are not likely to be sitting on our cushion in perfect meditation posture—likewise when the boss yells at us, when we crash our car or when our lover breaks up with us. We need to be able to use the skills we learn on the cushion at any and all points in our day. This is the practice of integration.

Integration as practice

Yes, integration is a practice in itself. The idea is that you do a formal session of meditation in the morning when you wake up, then you practice integration throughout the day. But even if you miss your formal session, you can still practice informally. However, it's a lot harder to integrate if you have no experience to integrate, so, ideally, informal practice should go hand in hand with formal sessions. In reality, whatever you can manage is fine, and anything is better than nothing, but don't fool yourself that informal practice is all you need. It isn't. If you want the benefits of meditation, then at some point you are going to have to do a good whack of formal practice.

Meditative experience accumulates

Trying to integrate meditation without having done formal sessions is like trying to fill a cup from an empty jug. The idea is that you fill the jug up in the morning, then you can pour yourself drinks throughout the day as you need it. Luckily, the meditation jug is a magical one; every moment you spend in meditation is stored in that jug and is never lost, so the more you meditate formally, the more you have to draw on when integrating.

You need to make an effort to consciously integrate. If you never try to integrate, you could meditate for years and not experience the real benefits, whereas if you consciously practise drawing your meditative experience and skills into your daily life, then the benefits will flow more quickly.

Ways to integrate

- Stop now and meditate—just take time to stop, breathe and centre yourself at any time during the day or night. Setting a timer on your phone is a good way to make sure this happens. I have a gong sound for text notifications, so whenever a text comes in, I have a moment of meditation.
- Always meditate for a moment whenever you sit. You're sitting anyway, so just take a few conscious breaths before doing whatever it was that you sat to do.

- Use difficult situations as a call to meditation, so if someone yells at you, you take a deep breath, then breathe out slowly, dropping all your reactions, thoughts and emotions as you do so. Just that much, an instant of letting go, makes a huge difference in your ability to handle difficult situations and people.
- Integrate loving kindness meditation by thinking to yourself: 'May you be happy; May you be well,' whenever you see another person, and particularly when you see another person who is suffering or in the grip of emotion. Sending them some loving kindness will open your heart so that you can also experience the benefit of feeling your own love.
- Healing meditation can be integrated in the shower. Imagine the water as liquid light that cleanses and heals you inside as well as outside. You can imagine each sip of water as healing nectar, building your immune system, and every shower of rain as healing nectar for the earth.

What Next?

Now you need to put what you've learned here into practice, and to do that fully, you'll probably need the assistance of a meditation teacher.

Why?

Because a book can't respond to you and your specific needs and issues. A live teacher can:

- answer your questions;
- check that you're practising correctly—an experienced teacher can tell by looking at you not only if your posture is good but also how your mind is;
- help you avoid pitfalls—our egos have many ways to trap us in delusion;
- help you to set up a program that works for you in your life;
- provide inspiration and encouragement;
- create personal programs for meditation and integration;
- create the right atmosphere for meditation.

These are all important points. It's too easy for us to find excuses for not practising and to get so caught up in stories about ourselves and our meditation that we can convince ourselves of almost anything, whether it's true or not. We need someone who can recognise and steer us past whatever obstacles arise, someone who can gently encourage us and give us solid support for our practice on both practical and motivational levels. There's nothing quite like sitting with someone who embodies meditation to help us embody it as well.

Because of the internet, you can have a meditation teacher no matter where you are. I had ten years of experience teaching meditation via Skype, and it's amazing how powerful an atmosphere can be created by meditating together on Skype. It's almost as if you're in the same room.

The internet takes away the issue of finding someone qualified in your area. Though it's great if you can find someone nearby whose approach you relate to, but this may not be possible. The internet offers more options. And the beauty of it is that you don't have to travel, and neither does your instructor; that makes it cheaper and easier to attend.

If you're interested in going to the source of my understanding, then you'll need to find yourself a teacher from the Tibetan Buddhist tradition, but be careful, some of them are abusive. Before looking stepping onto that path, please read my book *Fallout: Recovering from Abuse in Tibetan Buddhism.*

Whether you go for someone online, or in your area, or you're considering attending a meditation retreat, the following chapter is designed to help you evaluate a potential teacher.

How to Evaluate a Meditation Teacher

There are many different kinds of meditation, but the meditation teacher is just as important as the style of meditation, maybe even more so. So how do you find the best meditation teachers?

Whether you're looking for a meditation group in your area or looking for an online meditation teacher or course, the qualities to look for in a meditation teacher are the same.

The best meditation teachers:

- have been educated in meditation techniques;
- have been trained to teach meditation;
- have experience in teaching meditation;
- are kind, compassionate, relaxed and have a certain amount of wisdom; i.e., exhibit the kinds of qualities you'd expect to see in someone with a lot of meditation experience;
- are humble, not egotistical;

- will be able to create the atmosphere of meditation in their meditation sessions.

So how do you find out these things?

Look at the person's bio, but also read their blog posts. What they say in their bio will tell you the raw facts about them, but what they write and the way they write their blog posts—their voice and attitude—will tell you about them as a person.

Education

Look at who their teacher is. Is it someone well known in that tradition? How long have they studied with that teacher? Beware of anyone who doesn't say who their teacher was. Even the Buddha had teachers—he just surpassed their realisation. Meditation cannot be fully learned from a book, and a true student of meditation has great respect and appreciation for their teacher. After all, look what a gift they have given them—the knowledge of themselves.

Training

If the teacher belongs to an organisation, have they been trained within that organisation? Are they a recognised teacher or instructor within that organisation? And is it a reputable organisation or teacher?

Reputation

Google them. If there is a whiff of controversy, best stay away.

Experience

Everyone has to start somewhere, so someone with little or no experience can still be a good teacher, but there's nothing like experience to show you how to best explain something or help someone with a certain problem. So how long have they been instructing? And what kinds of instructing have they done?

Personal attributes

The latest scientific research on meditation and neuroplasticity shows that people who do a lot of meditation are happier, more compassionate, less prone to negative emotions and have a greater sense of empathy with others than those who haven't done a lot of meditation. And this is even when they aren't meditating. They also have less of a sense of separation from others, so are less inclined to prejudice and arrogance. Looking at this, it's clear that anyone who says that they are enlightened are most probably not. Even the Buddha didn't declare himself enlightened, his teachers did—they then became his first disciples. Enlightenment isn't one big bang, either. According to Buddhism, there are ten levels, or Bhumis, before you become fully enlightened. Anyone on any of those ten levels will not be strutting around declaring to everyone that they are enlightened. Nor will they be pushy and egotistical, or full of their own importance.

Atmosphere

The best meditation teachers create an atmosphere of peace and clarity simply by their very being because this sense of presence comes naturally to people with a lot of experience in meditation.

Make your own assessment

The only way to really know if someone is the right teacher for you or not is to go along with an open mind and see how you feel. You don't need to make up your mind right away. You can give it a bit of time.

I hope this will help you to evaluate the teachers on offer to you and find a teacher that is worthy of your diligence in following their instructions.

And Now ...

If you enjoyed this book, please help me out by taking the time to write a review and tell your friends about it. Not only do I love to hear what you think, but also your reviews and recommendations are a vital ingredient to help my books find readers.

Audio versions of the guided practices from this book can be found on Bandcamp in an album called Simply Being.

https://tahlianewland.bandcamp.com/album/simply-being-guided-meditation

Thanks to everyone who helped with this book especially to the teachers who provided me with such a comprehensive education in Buddhist philosophy and meditation.

About the Author

My social media bios summarise who I am by saying I'm an artist, author, editor, publisher and contemplative. I've written seven novels, a memoir of leaving my Buddhist group—*Fallout: Recovering from Abuse in Tibetan Buddhism*—and a book of writing tips—*The Elements of Active Prose*. My novels are fantasy and magical realism with a touch of romance, and a good dose of metaphysics.

My creativity also expresses itself in mask making, hat decoration (see TahliaMasks on Etsy) and animated AI art. (See my illustrated webbook *Psychemagination.net*, the self-examination journey of a late-diagnosed neurodivergent.)

Before becoming involved in the publishing industry, I had over twenty years' experience in scripting and performing in visual theatre and theatre in education. I'm a trained teacher and have taught in both primary and secondary schools.

I work as an editor for AIA Editing and Publishing and live in an Australian rainforest with a lovely husband and two cheeky Burmese cats.

Glossary

All unspecified references are from The Rigpa Wiki. http://www.rigpawiki.org/

Dharma: Put simply, the teachings of the Buddha. The word *dharma* comes from the ancient religions of India and is found in Hindu and Jain teachings as well as Buddhist. Its original meaning is something like "natural law". Its root word, *dham*, means "to uphold" or "to support". In this broad sense, common to many religious traditions, dharma is that which upholds the natural order of the universe.

http://buddhism.about.com/od/basicbuddhistteachings/a/What-Is-Dharma-In-Buddhism.htm

Dzogchen: The 'Great Perfection', or 'Great Completeness'. The practice of Dzogchen is the most ancient and direct stream of wisdom within the Buddhist tradition of Tibet. Sogyal Rinpoche describes it as "the heart-essence of all spiritual paths and the summit of an individual's spiritual evolution". As a way in which to realise the innermost nature of mind—that which we really are—Dzogchen is the clearest, most effective, and most relevant to the modern world.

Longchen Nyingtik Lineage: A Tibetan Buddhist cycle of teachings and practice.

Mahamudra: A body of teachings representing the culmination of all the practices of the Sarma schools of Tibetan Buddhism, who believe it to be the quintessential message of all of their sacred texts. The mudra portion denotes that in an adept's experience of reality, each phenomenon appears vividly, and the maha portion refers to the fact that it is beyond concept, imagination, and projection.]

Shedra: A centre of teaching. Traditionally this was in a monastery.

Vajrayana: The teaching, and practice, of the Vajrayana or 'Secret Mantra Vehicle' lies at the heart of the Mahayana Buddhist tradition of Tibet. Based on the motivation of bodhichitta—the wish to attain, for the sake of others, the state of complete enlightenment—the Vajrayana is a path centred on cultivating pure perception.

The Nature of Mind: The inseparable unity of awareness and emptiness, or clarity and emptiness, which is the basis for all the ordinary perceptions, thoughts and emotions.

www.ingramcontent.com/pod-product-compliance
Lightning Source LLC
Chambersburg PA
CBHW020653300426
44112CB00007B/369